Brownie Points

Bite-Size Life Lessons

June 1, 2016.

Joyce Turley

Joyce Turley

Published 2014 by Short Fuse Publishing
Copyright © 2014 Joyce Turley Nicholas

Interior Layout and Digital Design
by Imagine That! Studios
ISBN 978-1-937791-98-8

http://fuseliterary.com/short-fuse

Dedication

To the Turley and Nicholas families—how did I deserve two such wonderful clans?

Here are the two clans at the openings of Fred's building.

And to the women who have always supported my wild dreams: Lillian Boland, Darla Curry, Carol Goman, Marie Fedon, Helen Woskob, Georgia Kern, Elizabeth Julian, and Aileen Bridgewater. I wish you lived closer!

You have all been my "September Song" and I so enjoyed these precious days with you.

And to the most patient of them all, Laurie McLean. Short Fuse, your new publishing company is inspirational to so many toiling writers.

Table of Contents

Introduction

The ancient Greeks might have had the solution to managing their children's education. They baked sugar cookies in the shape of Greek letters, so their children could experience "the sweetness of learning."

When my son, Paul, was in the first grade, I baked brownies for him to take to school. There was a different spelling word iced onto the top of each brownie. The eager learners in his class wrote me a delightful thank-you note, claiming,

"After we had eaten all the brownie words, we all got 100 percent on our tests."

When I was in kindergarten, I walked around my neighborhood, knocking on doors, and ringing doorbells, and asking in a quizzical voice, "Yum-Yum?" My kind neighbors knew that I meant, "Do you have a cookie or a brownie for me?" That was the beginning of my sales career.

Then I came across an obstacle. Mom had pinned a mysterious note onto my sweater. Since I didn't know how to read yet, I continued on with my "begging scam." But this time when I knocked on the doors, the neighbors would say, "Sorry, Yum-Yum, we can't give you a brownie today, because your mother says you aren't eating your dinner."

Finally I realized that there was a correlation between the note pinned on my sweater and the fact that my neighbors were depriving me of brownies. I removed the note, and continued on my merry way.

Life can be so much more relaxed if we earn "brownie points" as we then get with the program. Here are my stories about this subject.

I have been handing out my homemade brownies to friends and business associates for years; I've made literally hundreds of batches of this favorite recipe. What a great way to earn brownie points -- for example, by distributing my brownies at a board meeting, and putting a smile on the faces of everyone in the room!

Please send me your stories after you show friends and strangers alike the sweetness of life by offering them your own special homemade brownies.

As Kahlil Gibran wrote in 1926 in his book Sand and Foam, "We shall never understand one another until we reduce the language to seven words."

Try these seven words: *I HAVE BAKED BROWNIES JUST FOR YOU!*

With sweet love,

Yum-Yum (Joyce Turley)

As my late husband Fred said once as we were doing the annual budget, "First item is brownies: $10,000!"

I never kept track of the costs. Some things are priceless.

Crumb of Wisdom

"Everyone comes from somewhere, and...everyone has a story."

—Movie reviewer
for the film *My One and Only*

Where Did Brownies Begin?

Springing from an old Scottish tradition, Brownies were good-natured little spirits or goblins of the fairy order. All were men and appeared only at night to perform good and helpful deeds.

Principally, only old women were now and then able to catch a glimpse of the goblin guests, called brownies, from the color brown. The brownie idea was woven into affairs of everyday life. People offered bits of food or drink in the corners of a room believing that good would come to their homes if the brownies were remembered.

The first chocolate brownies as we know them became popular at the turn of the 20th century with a recipe in the "Ladies Home Journal." The idea caught on mainly in the Chicago region. The magazine claimed that the chocolate helped support health circulation by keeping arteries flexible.

What was life like in the United States at the time brownies in chocolate form were introduced? US statistics report the following in 1905:

- The average life expectancy in the US was 47 years.

- Only 14 percent of the homes in the US had a bathtub.

- Only eight percent of the homes had a telephone.

- A three-minute call from Denver to New York City cost eleven dollars.

- There were only 8,000 cars in the US, and only 144 miles of paved roads.

- The maximum speed limit in most cities was 10 mph.

- Alabama, Mississippi, Iowa, and Tennessee were each more heavily populated than California.

- The tallest structure in the world was the Eiffel Tower.

- The average wage in the US was 22 cents per hour.

- The average US worker made between $200 and $400 per year.

- A competent accountant could expect to earn $2,000 per year, a dentist $2,500 per year, a veterinarian between $1,500 and $4,000 per year, and a mechanical engineer about $5,000 per year.

- More than 95 percent of all births in the US took place at home.

- 90 percent of all US doctors had no college education. Instead, they attended so-called medical schools, many of which were condemned in the press and by the government as "substandard."

- Sugar cost four cents a pound.

- Eggs were 14 cents a dozen.

- Coffee was 15 cents a pound.

- Most women only washed their hair once a month, and used borax or egg yolks for shampoo.

- Canada passed a law that prohibited poor people from entering into their country for any reason.

- Five leading causes of death in the US were: Pneumonia and influenza, tuberculosis, diarrhea, heart disease, and stroke.

- The American flag had 45 stars.

- Arizona, Oklahoma, New Mexico, Hawaii, and Alaska hadn't been admitted to the Union yet.

- The population of Las Vegas, Nevada, was only 30.

- Crossword puzzles, canned beer, and iced tea hadn't been invented yet.

- There was no Mother's Day or Father's Day.

- Two out of every 10 US adults couldn't read or write.

- Only six percent of all Americans had graduated from high school.

- Marijuana, heroin, and morphine were all available over the counter at the local corner drugstores. Back then a pharmacist said, "Heroin clears the complexion, gives buoyancy to the mind, regulates the stomach and bowels, and is, in fact, a perfect guardian of health."

- 18 percent of households in the US had at least one full-time servant or domestic help.

- There were about 230 reported murders in the entire US

The Best
Potato Salad
Recipe Ever

Speaking of the 1900s, potato salad has been a staple at picnics and parties for more than a century. Here's a recipe that many have told me is the best in the land. It's very fattening. Do. Not. Eat!

Ingredients:

6 medium potatoes, cooked and diced, then cooled.

1 large onion, chopped fine

Dressing:

1 cup whipping cream

1 Tablespoon prepared mustard

4 chopped hard-boiled eggs

1-1/2 cups Miracle Whip (or mayonnaise)

¼ cup chopped sweet pickles

½ teaspoon sugar

½ cup celery, chopped fine

½ cup green pepper, chopped fine

salt and pepper to taste

Whip cream, gradually whipping in Miracle Whip. Add sugar, salt, mustard, pickle, eggs, and celery. Mix in potatoes, onion, and green pepper a spoonful at a time so each piece will be coated with dressing. Chill in the refrigerator several hours before serving. The mixture will be very moist until set.

Spin The World.
I Want To Get On!!

A long time ago: a long, long time ago when I was about five years old, I went to my father and said, "I want to go to New Ork." He replied, "When you can say New York correctly, I will take you there." He didn't offer to help me with the pronunciation and walked away.

I went across the alley and knocked on the door where two old maiden ladies were living and asked, "Will you teach me to say New Ork?" After much practice with this speech block, I went back to Dad and asked, "Will you take me to New York?" He replied, "Yes, next week we will take the train to New York and then we will go over to Coney Island and buy a hot dog." To this day, hot dogs are one of my favorites—after brownies that is.

Lessons learned: Number 1, we must earn our rewards; number 2, a promise must be kept.

We lived in a small, slow motion town in Eastern Pennsylvania. A great place, but one that if your doctor gave you six months to live, you'd go there because it would seem like six years. On this important day, we traveled for two and a half hours on the Lehigh Valley Railroad from Pennsylvania to the big city, and disembarked at Grand Central Station in the very heart of New York. I was wearing my new white hat, or tam as they were called, and we strolled down to the Empire State Building.

I looked up with my head tilted way back. I had never seen anything so magnificent! "I am looking at the tallest building in the world." In my young mind, I also thought, "There is another big world out there that is different from the little town where I live. The world is spinning and I want to get on." I was so fascinated that my hat fell off while I was looking up in wonderment.

After walking many more blocks, my father said, "You lost your hat back on the steps of the Empire State Building. Boy, we're not going to win brownie points with your mother." I replied with, "Don't worry. Next time I come to New York, I'll find it." Over the years, I have been in New York many times, but I never tried to find my tam.

Years later, after teaching as a speech pathologist in one room school houses all the way up to top private schools, I decided to form my own seminar company and market my skills to top and middle management in various industries. My main topics were speed reading and presentation skills. It was fascinating and I was fortunate to get contracts in many of the Fortune 1000 companies throughout the United States and in twenty-four countries. My world was spinning! I also employed teachers, and met so many wonderful clients who became my extended family. I soon realized that if you like what you're doing, you'll never work a day in your life. I made such a game out of it. When I went to the different cities, I tried to take in everything by finding out what made the company tick and what made their community interesting. I learned that everything and everyone are important. Where else could I go on rides with my Disney clients and hear about engineering problems related to building Disneyland in France? Where else could I be taken through the plant of Binney & Smith and watch the beautiful colors in large white vats and see Crayolas being made? How about Mrs. Field's cookies? Debbie personally delivered a new cookie she was testing as I looked out from the classroom and watched the skiers in Park City, Utah.

Oh, to roam through the various auto industry plants and really learn why we need the Environmental Protection Agency. At another time, my main client was the U. S. Chamber of Commerce, located across from the White House. I had the privilege of visiting Washington often, teaching various associations, including the White House staff. I even met the barber who served four presidents. The entire nation was discussing President Reagan, and yes, I got the whole story! Did he or didn't he? The barber told me: President Reagan didn't color his hair, but had his hair trimmed every twelfth day in order to always look the same for interviews.

My contract with the Institute for Organizational Management often took me to college campuses for two-day courses. I went into every student union, college bookstore, and other locations that made their campus special, like the grotto at Notre Dame where I lit a candle each year for twenty years. Also at Notre Dame is the famous "Touchdown Jesus" stained glass. This is a large, beautiful stained glass of Jesus with upraised arms, and you can see it from both the football field, and the tennis courts where I sometimes played. It was also fun to work in the Stanford Law Building. This work led to some educational films that I did for them.

Chicago was one of my favorite cities; I had a client on The Loop. The little towns were the greatest where I was told about all the local characters and action "behind the scenes."

Then, I conducted a study on the relationship of athletic ability and speed reading, and worked in the basketball camps with Johnny Wooden, Rick Barry, Bill Sharman, and the Billy Jean King Tennis Camps.

I heard people talking about management skill: management by objectives, management by walking around, management by control. What ever happened to management from the heart? Give me a break! I started "management by brownies" and every time I went into a company meeting or board meeting, I took homemade brownies. The message was, "You are important. I baked brownies just for you." We started off the meeting right—with sweetness.

A few years ago, I bought a hot dog at an outdoor stand on the main street at Penn State.

The owner of the little operation was an eighty-six year old man with a big smile. It was a little chilly that time of year, so he was dressed in several layers of clothing. He told me that he works every day from 10:30 a.m. until 2:30 p.m. for seven or eight months a year. He used to be in the restaurant business, but said he likes the hot dog stand better than playing golf and loves all the college students. His tip jar was overflowing. He gave tips to charity. For 9/11 he collected over $1,700, and currently he helps with flood relief through the Red Cross. That many hot dogs sold and contributions from college kids' allowance! Why can he stand out in the cold with a smile? Because he likes what he is doing.

Safeway is a great example of a company that hires people who like what they are doing, plus they have a terrific training program. At my Safeway market in Strawberry, California, each checker asks you by name after they study it on the credit slip, "Mrs. Turley, would you like help out with your groceries?" Their clerks in the aisles ask if you are finding things or need help. Just yesterday, I asked the clerk if she likes the remodeling that the store did. Her reply was, "Of course, I love being sent to this store. It's so cheerful and the customers are great." If she didn't like what she was doing, she had me fooled.

Oh, the value of a smile when you are talking to clients in person or on the telephone. A smile is heard over the telephone. So is the optimum pitch heard on the telephone. Try this exercise, softly to yourself: say "Um-hmmm, um-hmmm," as if you are agreeing with a person. Then say, "Good morning." The pitch is so much more pleasing.

After some years, I wanted my world to spin even faster. I needed to go international and learn about the rest of the world, so I was fortunate to get hired to lecture on five cruise ship lines. My main motivation was a bonus for my teachers and their partners, since they allowed us to take one guest. My main ship was the QE2, but I also lectured on the maiden voyage of the SS Norway, where we hung out with the King of Norway, Jimmy Kirkwood who wrote "A Chorus Line," and Flip Wilson, a leading comedian of the day. Other lecturers estimated that stock brokers who presented onboard ship gained two new clients on a one-week cruise.

Many of the passengers were retired, so we

didn't make many contacts for company classes, but one day on the world cruise, I stopped in Hong Kong and was hired by the American Chamber of Hong Kong, which made connections for all the multinational training programs. It was wonderful, what I learned over lunch about the great companies in the world. This lasted for fourteen years and I flew over twice or three times a year for two-week engagements. Hong Kong has seven million people, but only a small percentage actually run the place. Since I taught about two hundred top management people on each visit, I knew more people going down the street than I do at home in California.

By listening to my clients, I learned so much about the twenty-four countries I worked in. How else would I know how to cross Canada by train, bus, car, and plane when I gave seminars in thirteen different cities? How else would I have the confidence to bungee jump outside of Queenstown, New Zealand? How else would I learn what really happened on Christmas Day in 1941 when Hong Kong fell to the Japanese?

Sometimes, when things were going too well, I would wonder if I were really worthy. My clients made me secure about this. One day, though, when I was working with the executives of a large Asian development company, on the top floor of a skyscraper, I looked down upon Hong Kong Harbor and thought, "I am working with these important people who are preparing to go into China to negotiate for billions of dollars, and do television interviews that scare them; Joyce, you are a phony." Then, on the other hand I thought, "Boy, if the old gang could see me now!" Do you ever get that feeling? Don't be hard on yourself. If you are standing there, you must have earned the opportunity!

Soon after, my world slowed, and wouldn't spin any longer. I was diagnosed with stage three cancer; a rare sarcoma in the thigh. The doctor said that my chance of surviving for another year was about fifty-fifty. There were several "cure" options, one of which included amputating my leg.

"Do you mean, Doctor, it's like flipping a coin for my life? Well, I take heads, and all of my friends will flip heads also." Would you believe it if I told you that many of the people I had worked with sent messages like, "I keep flipping a coin and it always comes up heads."

Where else could you get support like this other than family, friends, and associates? The next seven months, I tried to continue working, but it was difficult. When I was having the radiation treatments, and when the technicians would leave the room, I would close my eyes and visualize hiking in Nepal on a healthy leg. Two years later, my daughter and I hiked in Nepal. My leg did well for nine years and I was spinning my world as usual when one day, I walked across the room and my femur broke in half as a result of the radiation. In the fall, I broke my back and crushed two discs. I was so lucky that my husband was at home; he called 911 and we made it to the hospital without my bleeding to death. Again, the doctor said that a radiated leg doesn't always heal, and that amputation was an option once again. I refused. The rehabilitation took months, and I used a cane for two years. During rehabilitation, I again visualized that I was walking completely around the world on a good leg. A while later, my husband and I did just that. We flew to Oslo, then to the island of Spitzbergen, and then by helicopter to a Russian ice cutting ship, and cut through to the North Pole. We had one hundred and nine passengers from fourteen countries. We climbed down to the ice, and flew our respective flags. Oh, how proud I was of my American flag. We formed a circle, held hands, and walked completely around the world. If I had to describe eternity, this would be it—miles of flat ice.

This brings me full circle. Soon, I will pack some brownies and take them to friends in New York. I will walk, with a slight limp, to the Empire

State Building, which is no longer the tallest building in the world. There, symbolically, I will look for my tam. Whatever happened to it? Perhaps a little girl found it, wore it for years, and it went to hat heaven, never to be seen again.

I want to do it all over again, so I will walk over to Sak's Fifth Avenue and buy the most beautiful hat in the place. In fact, it won't be just a hat, but a "chapeau." Come by for a brownie and help me celebrate. Here are the stories that happened from my early life until now.

I No Marry You!

When Grandmother Graziella left southern Italy in 1888 at age fifteen, she was excited about meeting up with her brother and a possible future husband. She would begin a new life of opportunity in America.

As she left the port of Naples, there was her mama with tears in her eyes, waving goodbye. Graziella knew she would probably never see her mother again.

When she arrived at the Philadelphia Pier, she observed two young men running toward her. One was her brother whom she hadn't seen in five years. Brother Luigi embraced her and said,

"This is the man you will marry. He paid for your passage."

Graziella took one look and in Italian answered, "No way will I marry this man!" She couldn't speak English, couldn't read in either language, and had no money. However, she could go home with Luigi and help in his household.

Just a few months later the family drove two hours to Roseto, Pennsylvania for the religious festival called "The Big Time." The town is named after Roseto Valfortore, Italy, the birthplace of most of these citizens.

Luigi introduced Graziella to a handsome young man named Luciano. It was love at first sight. Luciano worked hard for a year in the dangerous slate quarry, paid the man back for the passage, and married the beautiful Graziella. They produced one son and four daughters and were part of the community in nearby Easton, Pennsylvania.

Graziella would walk miles around Easton to visit her friends, who had also sailed from Italy to establish a better life.

Graziella also loved new babies. So the young mothers would visit her with their new offspring. Graziella would comment, "Donna Bella. Do you give it the tit?" because she knew breastfeeding was the healthiest way to nourish a child.

For years the women would describe how Graziella would visit, always carrying a small basket covered with a white linen napkin. In the basket she had her homemade Italian cookies. She didn't call them brownies but everyone really anticipated her visit and surprises. Since Graziella couldn't read, she must have carried all her mother's recipes in her head.

Many years later, she stopped by my dad's house while I was home from college. "What do you study in the college, Joyce?" she asked. "Oh, you are going to learna the children to speak well and to read? That is wonderful. If you learna the people to read, they no be lonely!"

Grandmother never did read but to cover up her own loneliness, she put her energy into raising beautiful flowers to give to friends. They were her other "brownies" besides the cookies. Or was it her positive attitude and love of her new country that were the brownies she spread in her little American town?

Ragu Italiano

Grandmother made this wonderful sauce from memory, and I make it in my own home. When I visited Roseto Valfortore, they also made it in exactly this same way. The older Italian women keep a jar of this in their refrigerators so they can instantly treat you to pasta.

A mixture of meats gives this Italian sauce great taste. This makes enough for 2 pounds of pasta (your choice!)

Ingredients:

2 pounds of mixed meat (veal, pork, sausage, chicken, etc.)

2 six-ounce cans Italian tomato paste

1 can Italian plum tomatoes (2 lb. 3 oz.)

1 large onion, 2 cloves garlic, 1 Tablespoon chopped parsley

Put 3 tablespoons of olive oil in a Dutch oven and fry your choice of meats. Lift the meats out of pot and set aside. Add chopped onion and garlic to the pot. Sauté. Add tomato paste and fry for a few minutes, stirring, then fill the 2 empty tomato paste cans with water and slowly add to pot. Add crushed tomatoes and chopped parsley.

Simmer on low heat for one hour, stirring often. Add fried meats back in and cook slowly for 90 minutes. Taste for seasoning. If it's too tart add a tablespoon of sugar. If too thick, add a couple tablespoons of water.

And The Music Stopped

Adapted from a story written by Lynn Henriksen

Originally published in
TellTale Souls Writing the Mother Memoir

The music, mother playing classical music on our baby grand, lulled me to sleep every night of my life until I was 13-1/2 years old. And, in the middle of the night when the fairies dance, I dreamed of flying off with my mother to a happy place filled with nothing but sunshine and fun.

She had the prettiest teeth I have even seen. This five foot tall, free-spirited mother of mine was a brunette, a light-skinned, blue-eyed beauty, who didn't really look Italian. She got more than her share of attention from men. She made their heads turn when she walked into a room or down the street. I've often wondered if it was because she was so beautiful that she had such a love of beautiful things and wanted to make more of her place in life than it actually was. She instilled in me a love of music and art long before the music stopped.

By the time I was five years old, I remember wanting to be an actress, not a pianist, even though my mother had me playing a simplified version of Beethoven's "Minuet in G" by that time. Mother was a concert pianist on a small scale. Beyond giving me a classical piano lesson every day, she earned thirty-five cents an hour giving lessons in our house during The Great Depression, which she would take to the Savings & Loan to deposit in her "escape" account.

As I grew older, I remember playing duo piano, my treble to Mother's bass. We'd pound on the keys and I'd sing all the popular songs, and we had such fun. She was a happy lady, but complained about her marriage to my father. And, I have to say, I discovered she fibbed some to make her fantasy world more of a reality. She visualized a more intellectual life than she led. She wanted this life so badly that she made up a world in which she lived that wasn't exactly real. I think she always knew she'd make a major escape to be with people who had more of what she was interested in and where she could realize her dreams.

My father was proud of my mother for her refinement and attractiveness and musical talent, but he didn't know how to handle it or her, so he came off as domineering. In fact, I believe he thought he'd won the brass ring when my mother agreed to marry him. Sadly, it didn't take long for my mother to feel unhappily married, but she became pregnant with my older brother, so she stayed with my dad. He bought her an upright piano, which fit snugly against the living room wall, so she could lose herself in her music. That sufficed until the baby grand piano my grandmother actually bought me for my seventh birthday arrived and took up most of the room, and my mother took up all her spare time at the keyboard until the day the music stopped.

Pearl Harbor on the island of Oahu was bombed by the Japanese early one Sunday morning in December of 1941, shocking and shaking our nation momentarily to its knees. It ushered in the cacophony of World War II—a war that would last for four agonizing years. Just one month later, in the dusk of early night, one January evening of 1942, in Easton, Pennsylvania, my mother donned her black wool coat and tied a soft, silk scarf carefully around her hair before slipping soundlessly out of the house to go see Clark Gable at the movies. She'd mentioned earlier in the day that she planned to see a movie that evening after dinner. There were no good-byes to my father, brother, or to me. I went to bed in the quiet, no music by which to dream, unaware that my mother's music had stopped for all time in our old Pennsylvania house. She never came back.

She'd threatened to leave many times throughout the years, saying she'd take me with her, but my brother was to stay with our father. To say her abandonment brought me to my knees would not be true, since I told myself I believed she was a butterfly who needed to fly away. I knew she loved me. Somehow I understood something unspoken about her, but to this day I've always had to have a baby grand in my home whether or not I had the room or money for it, and even though I seldom play.

I don't know why she didn't take me with her, and I didn't ask her when she called several weeks after she left to ask me to pack her clothes and send them to her. I cleaned out my piggy bank to get the money, and because my instincts told me my father shouldn't know what was going on, I walked the twenty blocks, broken piggy in hand, to the post office to mail one brown cardboard box to an address in Danville, New Jersey I'd scribbled down. That was it, until almost four years later, when the Seventeen Magazine subscription was sent to me on my seventeenth birthday. I suspect that it came from her, even though the sender line was left blank.

Thirty years later I moved back to Pennsylvania from California, which was many years after I'd read the obituary a relative had sent me marking my mother's passing in Danville, New Jersey.

The obituary mentioned the generous donation my mother had made to her Catholic church by having bells built for it, replicating the bells she'd fallen in love with while teaching in Italy, on

My brother with our cat, Mama, and me...
before Mama left.

which I can only assume must have been one of her butterfly migrations.

One day soon after moving back East, my husband Fred and I were driving down the freeway when I noticed the Danville exit sign at exactly the same time my husband maneuvered to take the exit ramp. Obviously our thinking was in sync, we were headed for the church where she'd had the bells installed. Miraculously, as were drove up the lane, we heard music; the bells were ringing in all their glory. The saying rings true, this was music to my ears; music from my mother once again.

Fast forward another thirty years when I'm talking with our priest friend in Eureka, California, and he says, "My bells in the church have stopped ringing; the parishioners are sad that the music stopped." Fred and I looked at each other, once again in sync, knowing this was our cue. We would replicate these bells for our friend's Catholic church. The music of the bells is now ringing daily in honor of our mothers and of my late husband Fred.

My life is rich, full of travel, business, children and friends, and of this much I'm sure: whether

we have our mothers for thirteen years or sixty,
aren't we always sitting at the window waiting for
her to walk around the bend?

Hoorah!
Twinkies are back!

Having been raised by a bachelor father, our main cuisine consisted of Twinkies, Coca Cola and Campbell's soup. That was just fine with me. When I got very hungry, in the back of dad's store, I would make a ketchup sandwich. That was a piece of bread, butter, and ketchup spread on top. Later when I had kids, they couldn't believe I could eat such junk, but it fit my needs at the time. It was slightly sweet and filling.

There were also chocolate cookies in bins in the store and I used to steal my fair share of them. I think this was my first introduction to the idea of cookies, or brownies, as a reward.

People often ask me where I learned my public speaking skills. It was that same corner grocery store. I would have to say, "Good morning, may I help you?" I had to be accommodating and at the same time try to be interesting. So, as an adult, speaking came naturally, even if I had to say, "May I help you," to a thousand people in the audience.

Eventually, when I went off to college, guess what? We sat down to a meal three times a day. And it wasn't Twinkies and canned soup. I

Crumb of Wisdom

Work where you live; don't live where you work.

—Number One of Joyce's Lessons

had roast beef, mashed potatoes, salad, and a balanced meal. And the best part? I didn't have to cook anything.

My friends would complain and say, "I won't eat this slop. Let's go get a hamburger." I always stayed behind, because I thought I was at a banquet.

To this day I appreciate anybody who makes a meal for me and I feel that anyone who goes to a home cooked meal should always send a written thank you note to acknowledge their host's effort and caring.

When I married, ironically, I really got into cooking. My dear friend Lillian Boland and I put together the *As You Like It* cookbook, with profits going to charity. In the early 70s we were invited to cook on television. In those days there were no kitchens in studios, so we really had to improvise.

Here are a couple of our favorite recipes from the cookbook:

Trig's Crab Meat Delight

6 ounces Alaskan frozen crab meat (or canned)

½ cup celery, chopped

1/3 cup onion, chopped

Salt and pepper

Paprika

2 hard-boiled eggs

½ cup mayonnaise or salad dressing

Bread—rye, white, whole wheat or hamburger buns

Bacon

Sliced American cheese

Mix crab meat, celery, onions, seasonings, mayonnaise and eggs. Spoon on bread. Place one slice of cheese on top, then one strip of uncooked bacon. Broil until bubbly. Watch carefully. You can then keep in warm oven until ready to serve. You can also put this mixture on party rye for hot canapés at parties. Serves 4 or 5.

Brandy Herb Paté

1 lb chicken livers

6 oz. butter

1 onion, chopped

3 cloves garlic, minced

1 Tablespoon tarragon

1 Tablespoon thyme

1 Tablespoon oregano

1 teaspoon salt

1 Tablespoon pepper

1 bay leaf

¼ cup good quality Brandy

1 Tablespoon flour

Melt 4 oz. butter in skillet. Add onion and garlic. Sauté until soft and tender. Remove mixture from skillet. Add remaining 2 oz. butter to skillet and melt. Add livers and cook until browned. Add bay leaf, salt, pepper and herbs. Add flour and stir. Cover and cook about 5 minutes. Livers should still be slightly pink when cut. Combine onion mixture with livers and add brandy. Process in blender or processor. Cool mixture. Place in small bowl and store in refrigerator until chilled. Turn upside down and remove paté, keeping shape. Sprinkle parsley on top and around sides. Add flowers for presentation. Orange nasturtiums are colorful and can be eaten.

Seafood Lasagne

8 lasagne noodles

1 lg. onion, chopped

2 Tablespoons butter

1 8 oz. package cream cheese

1-1/2 cups ricotta cheese

1 egg, beaten

2 teaspoons dried basil

½ teaspoon salt

1/8 teaspoon pepper

2 cans condensed mushroom soup

1/3 cup milk

1/3 cup dry white wine

½ pound shrimp

½ pound crab (or artificial crab)

½ pound scallops

¼ cup Parmesan cheese

½ cup mozzarella cheese

Sauté onion in butter, put into a bowl, and add cream cheese, ricotta cheese, egg, basil, salt and pepper. In another bowl mix together mushroom soup, milk, wine, shrimp, crab meat, scallops and Parmesan cheese. Cook noodles until soft. Place a layer of noodles in casserole dish. Spread with half of first mixture and then top with one half of the second mixture. Repeat with remaining mixtures and noodles as before. Top with mozzarella cheese. Bake for one hour and fifteen minutes at 325°. Let stand for 10 minutes for cheeses to set before cutting.

The Value of a Thank You Note

In 1946, I received my acceptance to Penn State University. This was very exciting, but we knew that tuition would be a problem. My father delivered groceries from his store to the court house, and knew one of the state senators. My father asked Senator W if he had any senatorial scholarships to award. "I'm sorry, Trig, but I only get two a year and I've already given them out. But I wish Joyce good luck at Penn State." We were quite disappointed, and realized we'd have to find another way. A week passed, and my father received a phone call from the senator. "Trig, I could squeeze in a one semester scholarship; would that help you?" Father answered, "Of course, we are grateful for any assistance."

After I was in college for a few weeks, I bought a beautiful green and white card and wrote a thank you note, "Dear Senator, I love Penn State and I thank you for the tremendous opportunity. I promise to make you proud. Yours very truly, Joyce." The next time my father delivered at the courthouse, one of the secretaries informed him that the senator had received a letter from Joyce. This was a nice surprise for Dad. Several months went by, and the Senator called my Dad again. "Trig, I have stamped a four-year scholarship for Joyce because I feel that she will be a future leader." My twenty-five cent thank you card and my three-cent stamp, plus a father whom everyone liked, got me through college.

As the philosopher Omaraam Mikhael Aivanhov says:

There are all sorts of books which describe how to medicate and what formulas to pronounce during these medications. Do not deny that they are beautiful, useful, and effective. But there are two words which are never mentioned, words which for me are the most powerful of all, words; which clarify, which harmonize, and which heal, and these words are: "Thank You."

This story is full of figurative brownies—the senator's scholarship was a brownie to me; my thank-you note was a brownie sent back to the senator; and Trig's going to bat for his daughter was a brownie as well.

Crumb of Wisdom

"If the only prayer you said in your whole life was 'Thank you,' that would suffice."

—M. Eckhart, German Mystic

The Oil Boom: Midland, Texas

Crumb of Wisdom

"I've always been in the right place at the right time. Of course, I steered myself there."

—Bob Hope

Several months after marrying my first husband Mitchell, in 1951 we moved to Midland, Texas, so he could start his geology job with Shell Oil Company. Ranchers and oil executives mingled in this economic center of the Permian Basin, comprised of 62 counties throughout Texas and New Mexico. During this decade Midland quickly transformed itself from a small country town to a city with a skyline that earned it the nickname "Tall City of the Plains". But in 1951 it was still more cowboy town than oil town.

For the first two weeks we had to stay in the only local motel because there was no housing available in this emerging boomtown. In fact, the owner of the motel rented us his personal room and stayed elsewhere during that period. We finally found a duplex with an open gas heater and moved there. We were too young to care about the heater danger to the extent we should have. We were just happy to have a place we could call our own.

Since we only planned to be there for three months, I didn't apply for a teaching position, but I needed to get some kind of job. In this big desert there would have been absolutely nothing for me to do during the day if I didn't work. I felt like a real pioneer.

Midland was growing so fast, the infrastructure could not keep up. 215 oil companies had offices in Midland. Water for washing cars and watering yards was rationed on an every other day schedule. There were no trees or foliage so when the wind blew hard the dust storms swept people off their feet. At 105 pounds, it literally took my breath away. The dust got in my mouth and stained all our clothes. The department stores often had a half-inch of sand on the floor. It was the real desert.

The buildings were mostly one-story when we arrived, except for one luxury hotel, and a growing skyline. Not all the streets were paved. The only entertainment we had was driving about 20 miles to Odessa to the movies. There was no television, but we listened to our radio at night.

The only thing the men did was drink liquor. You didn't see many women in the saloons, though. There were parties in homes. But that was it for entertainment.

One day I was walking by this beautiful glass-fronted building located off the main street and I stopped to admire it. There was a help wanted sign in the window. It was a mapping reproduction company where the local oil executives would bring secret maps of their prospective oil fields for copying. We offered privacy. I interviewed for the job of receptionist and was hired immediately because I think I was the only college graduate to apply. Plus I was young and energetic.

My duties were to take the maps from the clients, have the reproduction specialists in the back copy the maps and then return them to their owners. This could take anywhere from a few minutes to a half hour depending on how many maps the oil people brought in. While this was happening, I had to entertain the clients by offering refreshments, magazines to read, and small talk.

One memorable client was George Herbert Walker Bush, who eventually became our country's 41st president. At that time he was the owner of his own oil company in Midland. He often sent other people so I only met him once, but I remember his smile and we discovered we had the same birthday in June.

Another memory was when I was put in charge of organizing the company's unlimited-budget Christmas party that year. I retained the nicest hotel in Midland, the Scharbauer Hotel, to cater this shindig and the food was exotic and plentiful. One of the guests was actress Greer Garson's husband. That was a thrill.

The owner of the company was a woman, a rarity those days. It was rumored that she had murdered her husband and inherited the company. This happened in the late 40s, and at that time a poor little helpless woman could get away with murder.

But a job was a job.

One day I want to return and see how things have changed. Bucket list.

The One Room Schoolhouse

Crumb of Wisdom

"Man's mind, stretched to a new idea, never goes back to its original dimension."

—Oliver Wendell Holmes

Right after college I went to work as an intern at a deaf camp for pre-school children and their mothers. It was an Easter Seals camp in Somerset, Pennsylvania.

As a speech therapy major, we were in charge of making lesson plans for the mothers to help them teach their deaf children.

That's where I learned the great lesson of patience. Sometimes we'd work weeks to have one word produced.

After this summer internship was over, I took a job in Cumberland, Maryland as a speech therapist.

This was my first adventure away from home. I had two roommates who were also teachers, and we made so little money we had to really budget. We used envelopes to store our cash for weekly rent, groceries, etc. and whoever had to do the grocery shopping or pay the rent took the money from the appropriate envelope. This way we didn't have to pay bank fees.

That winter we experienced the coldest winter on record. My old jalopy got stuck in snowdrifts many times. When I went to the school in Midland, Maryland, the Kraft cheese man who had the same route had to rescue my car from a snowdrift three Fridays in a row!

I then went on to teach at a top private country day school. I enjoyed both environments equally as well.

What a nice study this was for me in how

people handle life.

Crumb of Wisdom

"Nothing's impossible; the word itself says 'I'm possible.'"

—Audrey Hepburn

Children Love Brownies

All kids love to make brownies. And eat them! I have three children and four stepchildren. The stepchildren were also raised by a single parent, who later became my dear second husband, Fred. Here's a brownie for Reed, Kim and Paul Turley, plus Matt, Heidi, Marj and Kurt Nicholas.

Sophisticated Paul

When Paul was four or five, I practiced with him to answer the telephone. When my friend Bob called, he heard this young voice say, "Turley residence, Paul speaking," Bob thought to himself, "What a sophisticated little boy!" Then Bob asked, "Paul, where is your mama?" Paul answered, "Oh, mama went to the 'boody' shop!" Bob's idea of a sophisticated little boy reverted back to the toddler that he knew.

Fashion Conscious Kim

We had Kim's fifth birthday party in Oklahoma City where she was born. The day after the party I said to Kim, "Weren't the little girls adorable in their party dresses?" Kim answered in all innocence, "Yes, but Julie said she had the prettiest dress there and that's not true. Mine was the prettiest. I know because I looked!" Wouldn't it be great if our self-image were so positive that we always think we have the prettiest dress?

I'll Give You a 'Tiss

Paul Turley loved his brownies, and when I would tell him he could not have another one, he'd say, "If you give me a brownie, I'll give you a 'tiss." He had something I wanted and I had something he wanted. Do negotiating skills start at age two?

The Ten-Minute Philosophy

"Sorry, Paul, but you're going to have to wake up and get out of bed. I have to take the big kids to school and can't leave you home alone. I hate to do this, but we'll do something nice like make brownies when we come home." I had such guilt having to awaken a beautiful, sleeping child. Paul rubbed his eyes and said, "Oh, it's okay, in ten minutes I'll be happy." At three years old, he realized that sometimes things are tough, but with patience, we wake up to something good. Could we all consider the ten-minute philosophy? Wouldn't it be nice if, as adults, we could adopt this attitude? Knowing that even though the present moment may not be pleasant, with patience, we will see the sun shine again.

Crumb of Wisdom

"Home is the place where, when you have to go there, they have to take you in."

—Robert Frost

Come Home Reed

We lived on an acre of land in Oklahoma City beside a lake. One day in the backyard, Reed wasn't happy with what we were doing, and so he proclaimed, "I'm going to run away. Goodbye." He ran down to the bottom of the property. It took him awhile on his short legs. When he got there he turned and yelled back, "Do you miss me?" We answered, "Of course, Reed, we miss you! Come back, come back!" Perhaps we all need to run away for a few minutes, but don't forget to come back.

Paul Turley, age 9, with his dog Rimsky Korsakov

Crumb of Wisdom

"Any woman who understands the problems of running a home will be nearer to understanding the problems of running a country."

—Margaret Thatcher

UPS

When my granddaughter was a pre-schooler, she went to daycare every day since both her parents worked. This disturbed her grandma a bit, because I wasn't sure she was getting enough attention.

So I started sending her a surprise package every Monday. Nothing like something good to start your week. In the package I always put a few brownies.

This got to be routine, and every time she saw the UPS truck delivering in the neighborhood or around town she'd say, "They're getting a package and brownies from Grandma Go-Go!" She thought the whole UPS system was mine!

Camp Paddle Trails

My children were at the age that they wanted to go to a good summer camp.

The one that they chose was out of my budget range, so I applied to be a camp counselor in charge of dramatics as a way to defray the cost so my kids could go. It involved putting on skits at campfires each evening and holding classes each day for elocution and speech improvement.

The only reason it was possible to do this was because my husband was on an oil project in Ohio so he wouldn't be at home anyway.

The four of us set out for Camp Paddle Trails on the Oklahoma-Arkansas state line. The average daily temperature in the summer months was a tad over 100 degrees. Fortunately, the library of University of Arkansas was twenty miles down the road and open during the summer, so I would sneak down there to do my skit research during their nap time during the day. Then, I'd sit under a dull lamp outside my cabin when the campers were in bed, and would type the scripts on my loyal Royal portable typewriter.

My two older children were in different tribes. Five-year-old Paul had to stay in my cabin with me. He was in the Kickapoo tribe...the preschool group. It was the incorrigible Indian tribe.

It was the summer that one of the top selling songs was Camp Granada. I did learn all the camp songs that were as enjoyable around the lunch tables as they were around the campfire at night.

This was a very intense schedule for me, and when the bugler played Reveille in the morning, I felt like throwing a shoe at him. My friends from Oklahoma City all sent care packages during the eight weeks we were away from home. They were worried about my mental health, being gone for eight full weeks with over 100 kids. They even referred me to a few psychologists! They had a great time gossiping about Joyce at camp. I'm afraid it was at my expense.

My kids had a great time sailing and being exposed to sports. The two camp leaders were Dr. and Mrs. Pickle, who really kept everybody moving. The only danger I knew of and could see were the occasional rattlesnakes that would slither into the cabin. Dr. Pickle would always come to the rescue.

My big danger was gaining weight because they served huge meals. The exception was sometimes the cooks couldn't get breakfast ready in time because they were hungover so we would just pull cereal out of the pantry.

Crumb of Wisdom

"It's never too late to have a happy childhood."

—Unknown

Oh Camp Paddle Trails

Hats off to you.

To Camp Paddle Trails

We will be true.

I guess the lyrics of the songs really got to me, because next week one of the former adult camp counselors, the sports director, is coming to see me in San Francisco. She is now 86. Hats off to Anne!

Speed Reading Brownies

It was a cold, rainy January night in Oklahoma City in the mid-1960's, and I saw an advertisement to attend a free speed-reading demo put on by Evelyn Wood Reading Dynamics.

It would have been easier to stay at home before the television but I was taking post master credits at the University of Oklahoma and really needed the skill to move on.

Since the weather was bad, just a few attended the demo put on by franchise owner Lanny Curry. Ordinarily, I would have left after the introductory demonstration since I couldn't afford the $175 for the eight-week program. Lanny and I started talking and he offered me a job giving the demos in exchange for the course. (What a brownie gift.)

The rest is history. I taught the course for a year under Lanny but by then he had an opportunity to move up and moved to Tennessee. I took over for him and then started my own company, Dimensional Reading Inc. I moved the new office to the California Bay area and my teachers and I gave the Dimensional Reading course in forty-eight states and twenty-four foreign countries. We lectured on cruise ships, which gave us the opportunity to teach abroad.

I do have a book "Speed Reading in Business" by Crisp Publications, but here are the tips I give when I speak at conventions. The topic is "In One Hour, Double Your Reading Rate for Life."

The average person reads an average of 250 to 300 words per minute. If you can double that, and you read two hours a day, you'll cut it down to one, and you'll save seven hours a week for the rest of your life.

Anyone can learn to read faster by following our program. You don't need a high IQ. We don't stress sensationalism like some other speed-reading courses. And we stress what the average person can accomplish very easily.

If a person follows these rules, there's no way that, within a month, a person can't be reading light material at the rate of 800 to 1,000 words a minute, with better comprehension.

Here are my suggestions:

1. Use the hand as a pacer as you read. With the index finger or the middle finger or with both, slide you hand under each line from left to right. If there are just one or two words in a line, slide under the entire line since rhythm is important. Do this for a week or so.

2. As you become more proficient, vary your hand movement by going from left to right under one line, and right to left under the next two or three— you're not reading backwards, you're looking at the whole picture instead of worshipping the word. It's a feeling. You'll be developing peripheral vision, and it'll start falling into place. You'll have fewer eye fixations per page.

3. After another week or so, use a jogging method. With one or two fingers go down the page in an "S" pattern. Go at your own pace. At first you think, "I'm not getting anywhere," but it soon begins to fall into place. If it gets too tough, go back to step one or two until you feel comfortable again, and then try it once more.

4. Nag yourself. Every day, nag or push yourself to read faster than you're comfortable with for 15 minutes. It's a matter of building confidence.

5. To stop vocalizing or saying the words, distract yourself by sucking on candy or chewing gum, or even biting on a pencil.

6. Don't let your eyes linger on every word. When you look at a picture, you don't way, "There is the sky, the ground, the girl, the lawn, etc."—you look and get the message. Apply this to reading—simply train yourself to look at the printed page and get the message.

7. Increase your concentration by putting on earphones and turning on non-vocal background music loud and zero in on the printed page and block out everything else. Turning up the stereo won't do it. You need earphones. If you don't have earphones, you can get almost the same effect by simply humming loudly—not a tune—just a loud "h-m-m-m-m." It's almost a form of meditation, and it helps you concentrate on the printed page.

Speed will vary with the individual. I tell people to set their own pace and go as fast as they are comfortable with.

If you need more help: spinworld@aol.com. Good reading!

Crumb of Wisdom

"If you're not learning, you're not living."

—Craig Harrison

The Virginia Slims Experience

In December of 1969 the family was making plans for our Christmas vacation. My first husband and our three children were all avid skiers, but I was a coward and didn't enjoy skiing that much.

I said, "Kids, I'm going to go to a tennis clinic in Honolulu put on by Billie Jean King. I know you don't know her but she won Wimbledon this year. You can come to either the tennis clinic with me or go skiing with your dad. It's up to you."

They all chose skiing, so I started out for Hawaii by myself.

Since I was traveling alone, Billie Jean King, her husband at the time, Larry, and world-renown tennis coach Dennis Van Der Meer, invited me to join them for dinner after the lessons each day. By New Year's Eve we had become great friends and I offered to arrange tennis clinics for them in Oklahoma City. In return they invited me to conduct speed reading classes at their California and Nevada tennis camps. For the next year they made several visits to Oklahoma and everyone in town enjoyed their appearances at our little tennis club. Tennis was just becoming popular there, so it was an exciting time to be associated with the sport. We had a lot of fun.

A year later I received a phone call from Billie Jean saying, "The girls have broken away from the boys in tennis and we're starting our own league. The Philip Morris Company is marketing their Virginia Slims brand of cigarettes to women and has agreed to sponsor a series of women-only tennis tournaments in twelve cities, including Oklahoma City. Their motto is: 'You've come a long way, baby.' Would you be the director for the Oklahoma City tournament?"

"Billie Jean," I said, "you know I was your worst student. I don't know the difference between a tennis racquet and a baseball bat. How can I do this?"

She told me that she only needed someone who was visible in her community and they had selected Oklahoma City as one of the first tournament stops.

"Larry, Dennis and the Ruder Finn publicity firm in New York will give you a lot of help," she said.

I agreed, but only if my co-director could be Suzanne Mears. Together we made a good team. Suzanne contributed the artistic flair that complemented my business acumen. We only had three months to pull this event together, including securing 100 sponsors, so we both worked 16-hour days as a matter of course, and went way beyond our comfort levels often. I had never experienced such a big challenge before. I even loaned them $1,500 from my savings account to get the ball rolling.

In January, in the midst of the infamous Oklahoma storms, we made history.

The night before the tournament, we had the turf tennis court flown in and many volunteers helped install it in the Oklahoma City University field house.

The tennis women really stepped up their game. When Billie Jean, Rosie Casals, Francois Durr, Judy Dalton and the rest of the top 16 women tennis players in the world arrived, they gave media interviews everywhere and spoke at high school assemblies. They even agreed to be billeted in private homes throughout the city instead of the hotels they were used to staying in when they traveled. And they endured the endless parties Oklahoma threw in their honor.

I worked my head off securing sponsors and even convinced the governor of Oklahoma to throw out the first ball to start the tournament. Many volunteers put up tennis flyers all over town. Volunteers also chauffeured, ushered, entertained, ran errands, sent mailings, stuffed envelopes, and so much more. My co-director Suzanne designed the 16 wonderful billboards placed all over town. And we even had a roast-beef press conference put on by Ruder Finn that attracted media from all over the state. It was unheard of at the time to have a full luncheon for the press, so the roast beef might have helped gather so many reporters. We ultimately scored more column inches of publicity than the University of Oklahoma football team—an amazing

feat since the football team garnered more news stories than any other sport every year.

The Oklahoma City first Virginia Slims Women's Tennis tournament was a huge success. Everyone in town came to the week-long sold out event. Billie Jean won the tournament and received $2,500 in prize money—the highest amount ever earned by a woman in a tennis tournament. That included Wimbledon.

We made a whopping profit of $280. I was repaid my loan, and the $280 went to the Oklahoma City University boy's tennis team. There was no Oklahoma City University girl's tennis team at the time. There is now.

The following year was even more of a success. The top 32 players competed, our profits greatly increased, and journalists competed for an invitation to our legendary roast beef press conference.

As a reward for a job well done I was invited to attend both the U.S. Open at Flushing Meadows in New York and Wimbledon in England. One of my most memorable moments was going to the Wimbledon party held before the activities began. I stood at the top of the stairs in my full-length gown as they announced my name, but before I could make my Cinderella-like grand entrance down the stairs one of the Ruder Finn guys yelled out, "Joyce, baby! You've come a long way." I rolled my eyes, shushed them, and proceeded down the stairs anyway.

At the Wimbledon tournament, former Wimbledon winner Ann Hayden Jones gave me her center court tickets, which she couldn't use because she was the BBC announcer that week. Her husband Pip took me into the most exclusive tennis club in the world: the All English Tennis Club. "Not even the American press corps is allowed in here," Pip said. He introduced me to a group of sophisticated English ladies. They had a million questions to ask me about American tennis and Billie Jean's personal life, which was a bit scandalous at the time because of a tell-all memoir she'd written. I just raved about how much Billie Jean had done for the world of women's tennis and steered clear of any conflict. Afterwards Pip whispered, "Job well done."

I would have organized more Virginia Slims tournaments, but I found myself single and moved to California the following year. There I kept up with my tennis cronies and continued teaching speed reading at their tennis camps. To this day we remain friends, and several years ago my daughter Kim and I attended The Billies, a charity event that Billie Jean put on at the Beverly Hilton.

Throw your ball into the universe! You never know where it's going to land. Things don't happen while watching television in your living room. You have to be out among them.

Crumb of Wisdom

"You've come a long way, baby."

—Motto of the *Virginia Slims* cigarettes

Right Was Right

Dimensional Reading Inc. was a new company I started in 1971. The office was in Oklahoma City where I had been co-director for the Oklahoma Virginia Slims tennis tournaments.

As a result of the first successful season, Billy Jean King became fascinated when I gave speed reading demos to the tennis stars. She was an avid reader and invited us to teach speed reading in her West Coast and Nevada tennis camps.

The owner of the John Wooden, Bill Sharman, and Rick Barry basketball camps heard about it and called, asking me to meet with him in Mill Valley, California to discuss presenting lectures as an elective during their camping season.

Billie Jean King takes speed reading lessons from Joyce Turley.

I flew to San Francisco, borrowed a car from a friend, and drove across the Golden Gate Bridge to present my pitch.

The president of the camps became interested and hired me to give seminars the very next summer. I was thrilled, left his office and drove right to get on to Route 101 South to return the car to San Francisco. I should have turned left. After several miles I found myself in a town called Tiburon. What a beautiful, European-like seaside village.

That's it! Here, I will establish a wonderful home for my three children and me. I flew back to Oklahoma, packed up our things, and made sure the older two kids were settled at the University of Oklahoma.

Paul was in tenth grade and we made the move together to our new home in the West.

The entire plan took six months. On a quick familiarization trip to Tiburon I tried to rent an apartment I could afford. The owner wouldn't allow teenagers!

I then had letters of recommendation sent from friends and teachers stating that Paul would be an asset to the complex since he was very responsible and would help the tenants.

Finally, the owner said that my son and I could rent. My reply was, "No, we will find a friendly place that is more beautiful than this. You can rent to old folks."

Of course the rent was much higher but I decided I'd just work harder. We unpacked, baked homemade brownies, and on the ninth day put an invitation in every neighbor's mail box (about twelve).

"We aren't completely settled but hope you will stop by on Saturday afternoon for Champagne, hot dogs, and brownies," signed, "Your new neighbors: Joyce and son Paul." What a neighborhood it turned out to be! The people were so friendly and welcomed us to the area. The one neighbor was also a Penn State graduate and offered to introduce me to someone in the Standard Oil of California's training department. Another neighbor opened the door for me at one of the top banks; another, a contact at Stanford to produce a training film.

I used the house on the water to train new teachers, give classes on Saturday mornings, and the neighbors never complained that my pupils parked for a Saturday class. Instead they would say, "You had a full class today. Good for you!"

Crumb of Wisdom

Never "next-time" anything.

There are just so many tomorrows.

—Number Two of Joyce's Lessons

Golden Gate Brownies!

On St. Patrick's Day 1975, my 16-year-old son and I left Oklahoma City to establish a home and new speaking business in Tiburon. It was time to leave some memories behind. We knew no one, and Paul was a day late in enrolling in his new high school because I couldn't find Larkspur.

A few days later I was driving south over the bridge to call on my first company but I was not sure of directions, where to park, and had no extra jacket for the wind and chilly San Francisco temperatures I was not yet accustomed to. I might say that the responsibilities I had set up for myself were a bit overwhelming. With a tear in my eye, I stopped at the toll gate to give the young man my 75 cents when I heard a pleasant voice say, "Hello, lovely lady. What is your name?" He shook my hand and said, "Joyce, I am Paul Torrente and I want you to have a beautiful day." This was my welcome to the most magnificent bridge in the world from the wonderful people who were there greeting drivers. With those warm wishes, who wouldn't close her first sale for the new company?

As the business grew and I continued to cross the Golden Gate Bridge, I would tell them where I was going. I was crossing mainly to drive to the airport to speak in far away places. I crossed the bridge on my way to meet an old college friend who later became my husband. I crossed to attend parties, business meetings, birthdays, chemotherapy and radiation treatments, and open heart surgery while wondering if that would be my last crossing. Every time I had a house guest we walked across the bridge and admired the beautiful city. I still walk across every now and then, but just half way.

Then FasTrak was put in and I missed the people working in the tollbooths who make the bridge even more special, but some years later I started to stop at the booths again as I had to show my handicapped permit. I've been stopping at tollbooths for ten years now, usually for a quick visit, to give them a few of my homemade brownies, and to introduce them to my children or grandchildren. They put the recipe in their lounge with a note saying, "It is OK to eat Joyce's brownies." When my husband died they sent a sympathy card signed with notes from 20 of them.

I know that change is inevitable and now crossing the Golden Gate Bridge is automated and I will not be able to visit with the wonderful people in the tollbooths. Even though I am still crossing to catch planes to deliver my motivational convention speeches on longevity, I realize that since I am in my eighties now, one day I will have to hire a driver to drive me across the bridge. When we drive past the empty tollbooths we will hear their whispers in the wind:

"Hi, Joyce! Where are you off to? To the North Pole to walk around the world? We will be listening for your footsteps." "How are the grandchildren? Bring them next time." "We loved meeting your house guests from Hong Kong and hope they enjoyed their journey across the bridge." "We loved the brownies and have made them ourselves. Thanks for the recipe. Have a wonderful day and wonderful life."

Their kind words will stay with me always. For now, each year I will put a candle on a brownie and say, "Happy birthday, Golden Gate!" My conclusion after crossing the bridge for 37 years is this: On the inside, isn't everyone from a small town and aren't we all going across the bridge to find good things on the other side?

Crumb of Wisdom

"My two favorite four letter words are HOME and LOVE. Isn't the best part of any trip the minute you put the key in your own door?

—Joyce Turley

Golden Gate Bridge Facts

(from the San Francisco Travel Association)

Why the name Golden Gate?

The Golden Gate Strait is the entrance to the San Francisco Bay from the Pacific Ocean. The strait is approximately three-miles long by one-mile wide with currents ranging from 4.5 to 7.5 knots. It is generally accepted that the strait was named "Chrysopylae", or Golden Gate, by John

C. Fremont, Captain, topographical Engineers of the U.S. Army circa 1846. It reminded him of a harbor in Instanbul named Chrysoceras or Golden Horn.

How long did it take to build the bridge?

Just over four years. Construction commenced on January 5, 1933 and the Bridge was open to vehicular traffic on May 28, 1937.

When did the Golden Gate Bridge open?

The dream of spanning the Golden Gate Strait had been around for well over a century before the Golden Gate Bridge opened to traffic on May 28, 1937. Pedestrian Day was held on May 27, 1937.

Were hard hats used when building the bridge?

Yes they were and here is how they came to be. The E.D. Bullard Company was founded in 1898 in San Francisco, CA, where the firm manufactured equipment for miners in western states. Many years later when Bullard's son, Edward W. Bullard (1899-1963), returned from World War I, he applied his experience with Doughboy army helmets in designing protective headgear for miners, and soon after, for the construction industry. E.W. Bullard's original 1919 "Hard-Boiled Hat" was manufactured out of steamed canvas, glue and black paint and included a suspension device. It was considered the first "hard hat," which revolutionized construction and mine worker safety. During construction of the Golden Gate Bridge, Bullard adapted his hats for bridge workers. E.D. Bullard Co., Inc. remains a family-owned business and continues to produce innovative products for construction and public safety from its headquarters in Cynthiana, Ky.

How many workers died during the construction of the bridge and what were their names?

Eleven men. Until February 17, 1937, there had been only one fatality, setting a new all-time record in a field where one man killed for every million dollars spent had been the norm. On February 17, ten more men lost their lives when a section of scaffold carrying twelve men fell through the safety net. October 21, 1936: Kermit Moore February 17, 1937: O.A. Anderson; Chris Anderson; William Bass; O. Desper; Fred Dümmatzen; Terence Hallinan; Eldridge Hillen; Charles Lindros; Jack Norman; and Louis Russell.

What's the Halfway-to-Hell-Club?

The most conspicuous precaution was the safety net, suspended under the floor of the Bridge from end to end. During construction, the net saved the lives of 19 men who became known as the "Half-Way-to-Hell Club."

What would it cost to build the bridge today?

The cost to construct a new Golden Gate Bridge would be approximately $1.2 billion in 2003 dollars. The total price depends on a many factors including the extent of the environmental reviews and the cost of labor and materials.

How many rivets are there in each Golden Gate Bridge tower?

There are approximately 600,000 rivets in each tower.

What is the poem on the bridge written by Joseph B. Strauss?

Upon completion of building the Golden Gate Bridge in May 1937, Chief Engineer Joseph B. Strauss wrote a poem entitled "The Mighty Task is Done."

On opening day in 1937, how did the San Francisco *Chronicle* refer to the Golden Gate Bridge?

A thirty-five million dollar steel harp!

Why is the Golden Gate Bridge painted in international orange?

The Golden Gate Bridge has always been painted orange vermilion, deemed "International Orange." Rejecting carbon black and steel gray, Consulting Architect Irving Morrow selected the distinctive orange color because it blends well with the span's natural setting as it is a warm color consistent with the warm colors of the land masses in the setting as distinct from the cool colors of the sky and sea. It also provides enhanced visibility for passing ships. If the U.S. Navy had its way, the Bridge might have been painted black and yellow stripes to assure even greater visibility for passing ships.

Why isn't the Golden Gate Bridge painted gold?

Actually, the term Golden Gate refers to the Golden Gate Strait which is the entrance to the San Francisco Bay from the Pacific Ocean. The strait is approximately three-miles long by one-mile wide with currents ranging from 4.5 to 7.5 knots. It is generally accepted that the strait was named "Chrysopylae" or Golden Gate by Army Captain John C. Fremont, circa 1846. It is said it reminded him of a harbor in Istanbul named Chrysoceras or Golden Horn.

How often is it painted?

Many misconceptions exist about how often the Bridge is painted. Some say once every seven years, others say from end-to-end each year. Actually, the Bridge was painted when it was originally built. Until 1965, only touch up was required. In 1965, advancing corrosion sparked a program to remove the original lead-based paint (which was 68% red lead paste in a linseed oil carrier). The removal continued to 1995. In 1965, the original paint was replaced with an inorganic zinc silicate primer and acrylic emulsion

topcoat. In the 1980s, this paint system was replaced by a water-borne inorganic zinc primer and an acrylic topcoat. The Bridge will continue to require routine touch up painting on an on-going basis.

How many ironworkers and painters maintain the bridge?

Currently, a revered and rugged group of 13 ironworkers and 3 pusher ironworkers along with and 28 painters, 5 painter laborers, and a chief bridge painter battle wind, sea air and fog, often suspended high above the Gate, to repair corroding steel. Ironworkers replace corroding steel and rivets with high-strength steel bolts, make small fabrications for use on the Bridge, and assist painters with their rigging. Ironworkers also remove plates and bars to provide access for painters to the interiors of the columns and chords that make up the Bridge. Painters prepare all Bridge surfaces and repaint all corroded areas.

Has the Golden Gate Bridge ever been closed?

Yes, the Golden Gate Bridge has been closed due to weather conditions only three times: As gusting winds reached 69 miles per hour on December 1, 1951, the Bridge was closed for three hours. On December 23, 1982, high winds of up to 70 miles per hour closed the Bridge for almost two hours. The Bridge easily withstood the gusts. On December 3, 1983, once again high winds closed the Bridge for the longest period in its history, 3 hours and 27 minutes. Wind gusts reached 75 miles per hour, but again the Bridge suffered no structural damage. The Bridge was closed very briefly on two separate occasions for visiting dignitaries President Franklin D. Roosevelt and President Charles de Gaulle of France. It has also been closed briefly in the middle of the night for construction activities.

How many cars have crossed the Golden Gate Bridge?

As of April 2011, 1,929,896,448 vehicles have crossed the Golden Gate Bridge (includes northbound and southbound) since opening in 1937.

Is there anything special about the Golden Gate Bridge, like the shape, that influences the fog?

"Advection fog" forms when humid air from the Pacific Ocean swoops over the chilly California current flowing parallel to the coast. The fog hugs the ground and then the warm, moist air condenses as it moves across the bay or land. This is common near any coastline. The Bridge has an influence in directing the fog as it pushes up and pours down around the Bridge. Sometimes, high pressure squashes it close to the ground. By the way, the color of the bridge is International Orange, and was chosen in part because of its visibility in the fog.

What year did the Golden Gate Bridge appear on the cover of Rolling Stone Magazine?

On February 26, 1976, the Golden Gate Bridge appeared on the cover of Rolling Stone Magazine as the backdrop with five prominent San Francisco based rockers of the day, with a title above the photo that read, "What a Long Strange Trip it's Been."

San Quentin Brownies

telephone rings

"San Quentin? You want Adult Ed courses? I'll be there Friday night!"

Paul and I had just moved to California and I needed any job I could find, so every Friday night for six weeks I taught speed reading courses to twenty prisoners.

I had heard about the programs at San Quentin and loved the fact that I could earn a few extra dollars. I packed up the books, a few brownies (which was allowed in 1975, but no longer), and started out on a dark December night for the prison. It was cold and dreary. The wind was blustery, making me wonder what on earth I was doing. Boy, what a person has to do to pay the rent!

I left my son teenaged Paul back at the house and hoped I'd come home with some tales to tell him about my time in prison. He'd probably find it as uninteresting as any other class I returned from.

I was scared. What would I do in a closed classroom? Would they like me? Would I like them? I didn't want them to see my fear.

The guards didn't go into the classroom with me, but I was told to wear a blazer, so I could fit the panic box they gave me into my pocket and call a guard immediately if I needed help. One guard explained that this box was for my protection in case the inmates fought with each other. Somehow that didn't calm my fears all that much.

The room itself was a simple classroom, study chairs in rows facing me as I stood before them.

There was an older man that I paid special attention to because he was in his seventies and kind of frail. His name was Charlie and he always seemed excited to learn how to speed read. Finally I asked the guard why Charlie was in prison and his answer was that while naked, he had killed a man in Golden Gate Park. As weird as that seems, it didn't change my opinion of Charlie at all. I still gave him extra attention and he was polite and studious.

The classes were well received, the prisoners well behaved, and they tried hard to become prize speed readers so they could earn a brownie from the "outside".

I must admit I was sorry when the series of classes ended.

On the last evening I started to drive to the gate to go home. I saw flashing lights and heard the loud speaker system say: "Mrs. Turley, Mrs. Turley...wait at the gate please. Wait at the gate." I froze. It was so dark and frightening. There must be a prisoner in my back seat. Why else would they stop me? I didn't feel a gun at my neck. Perhaps that would be next.

I slowly approached the gate, lowered my window several inches to look at the guard. He came over and asked, "Mrs. Turley...I heard that you were recently the director of the Virginia Slims Tennis Tournament. Would you rally on the tennis court with me sometime?"

My response was, "Sure. Sure. Just call me. My number is in your records."

I drove through the gate and took my first breath on the way home. When I arrived, Paul asked, "Mom. Did you have an evening class some place in Marin tonight?"

"Oh, yes," I answered. "Just doing a little overtime in the classroom. Did you finish your homework? If you don't need any help, I think I'll go to bed!"

Crumb of Wisdom

"Just know that I am here, I care for you, and I have brownies."

—Madison Park Reading Company
Seattle, WA

One Dance In Life

Here's a brownie to one of my good friends. Sometimes the sweetness fades too fast.

It was 1960 and my French friend strolled down the street in Algiers. It was a difficult time for everyone as the Algerians were revolting against the French. They wanted to be independent.

Jeanne Marie worked in a perfume store. On the path she would often pass an exceptionally handsome young man. What a thrill to get a nod. "He must be the most charming man in the world," she thought. "If only I could meet him, but I'm much too shy to ever say a word to him."

This went on for months, scurrying to be in the right place at the right time so she could get a nod. The nods became "Bonsoir, Mademoiselle," and his blue eyes and smiles were unbelievable.

One Saturday afternoon, Jeanne Marie and a lady friend finally got the nerve to attend a dance at the hotel. They had heard about the afternoon affair for so long. It had a reputation as a place where singles could meet the single world.

They entered slowly, paid their entrance fee and watched the couples dance around the large ballroom. Jeanne Marie tried to act nonchalant, but really couldn't have the slightest hope that any man would invite her to whirl around the room. Just then she heard, "Mademoiselle, would you give me the pleasure of this dance?"

It was he!

"Oui, it would be a pleasure," she said automatically. "This can't be happening to me," she thought. "I'm actually in the arms of the most attractive man in all of Algiers. This is the man I dreamed about!" They had one, two, three, four minutes and she knew this was the beginning of her real life.

They whirled and turned so that Jeanne Marie was now facing the band and her partner had his back to them.

Suddenly she heard an explosion and screaming broke out. Panic! A terrorist's bomb had gone off and hit her partner in the back. Her life's dance partner fell dead in her arms.

Her first thought was, "I will never know your name!"

The pain of the event was overshadowed by pain in her right leg. Everyone s c r a m b l e d , pushing down the steps in the dark, trying to escape. Jeanne Marie woke up in the hospital to learn what had actually happened. But no one knew who the man was to be able to tell her whether he had actually died or not. She read

the list of victims in the newspaper, but since she didn't know his name, she had no idea how to find him or whether he was alive or dead. The shrapnel has remained in her leg for years.

Ten years later she moved to America and receives a monthly small check from the French government for her pain and suffering. Each time she goes to the mailbox to collect her check she is reminded of what could have been. She knows that the happenstance gave her happiness and tears for a lifetime. But I often wonder if Jeanne Marie's dream man is still out there, remembering their dance and wondering what happened to her. If you have heard this story from her dance partner's point of view, have him send me an email at spinworld@aol.com.

Crumb of Wisdom

"Live your life like an exclamation, not an explanation."

—Unknown

Second Time Around

After being a single mother for more than four years, I had a gig in Allentown, Pennsylvania and seminar assignments in four

other states the same week, so I planned to stop and visit my college roommate, Marie Fedon, while in Pennsylvania. I had forgotten how beautiful the East Coast was with all the fall colors, and I was feeling nostalgic.

She had tickets for the Penn State football weekend and invited our classmate to come and be my date.

Fred Nicholas walked across Marie's living the room, shook hands, and asked, "Remember me from the good old days? I hear you're living in California. You're having a big drought there, aren't you?"

"Oh, yes," I replied with a smile. "It's so bad we have shower with a friend."

His great sense of humor came through without missing a beat. "Oh, really? Could I come out for Thanksgiving?"

It was a super weekend visiting with old classmates, and Fred drove me around the town of State College, bringing me up to date with changes that had occurred since we'd graduated.

On Tuesday I reported to the Allentown Chamber of Commerce to present my program. There was Fred in the front row. I was so pleased that he wanted to learn how to speed read.

Then, on Wednesday, I traveled to the Chamber in Philadelphia. There was Fred in the front row again. I couldn't believe he'd spend money to repeat the course.

On Thursday I was in Washington, D.C., and once more Fred was in the front row. Friday, on to Rocky Mount, North Carolina and my star student still needed to polish his speed reading skills.

"My...am I being stalked?" I asked him. But in reality I was flattered.

We went out for a drink after class and hit it off so well I ended up inviting him to visit me in California for Thanksgiving. He agreed immediately. His excuse was that his daughter Heidi was attending UCLA and Tiburon would be a good meeting place for them both—even though there wasn't a speed reading course being offered there during the holidays. Both our families got along famously.

When he came back for Christmas he was finally ready to make his move. He told me, "Joyce, I've prepaid my staff for a month and told them I wouldn't be back in the office until I had closed the Turley account. We just must get married now. Besides I scanned the magazines in your living room and we subscribe to the same ones, so if we got married we could save a lot of money."

On January 3, 1977, we were married in Old St. Hilary's Church in Tiburon with just seven people plus the minister and his wife. There wasn't time to plan, as Fred needed to get back on the job in Pennsylvania. My son, Paul, was our best man and we had to wait until he got home from school for the ceremony to begin.

A month later we met each other's kids. Fred had raised four and I had three.

For 32 years we commuted between both coasts. It worked for us.

We traveled the world and had a wonderful life, learning from each other. The first year we were married, we had six out of our seven children in college. The adult children were soon out in the world and the two families blended well.

Today all seven kids, spouses, and 11 grandchildren are in and out of my life and I make brownies at least twice a week for the whole gang.

Joyce and Fred

Crumb of Wisdom

"What good are vitamins. Eat a lobster. Eat a pound of caviar. Live! If you are in love with a beautiful blond, with an empty face and no brains at all, don't be afraid, marry her. Live!"

—Arthur Rubenstein, at age 75

Thank you, Mr. Scott

I often spoke at conventions held at the Washington Hilton in the District of Columbia.

One day I was running late to speak to a large group of certified public accountants. It was the American CPA Association.

I went up to the hotel's registration desk to get a room key so I could change for the speech. They told me that there would be an hour's wait because Prime Minister Begin of Israel was at the hotel and they were very busy with security measures.

I was in panic mode, but went to the middle of the lobby and saw one of the bellman whom

I had spoken with before. I said, "Mr. Scott, how are you? And how is your wonderful son who was in medical school the last time I talked to you? Can you believe that I can't get a room and I'm going to be at the podium at 1:00?"

He said, "Oh, yes, Mrs. Turley from California. How are you? Please wait here for just a moment."

He returned in a few minutes with a key and said, "Young lady, you have a suite!"

I tried to tell him that I was only a breakout speaker, not a keynote, and I didn't deserve a suite.

As he led me to the most beautiful suite I'd ever seen in a hotel—two bedrooms, a full kitchen, beautiful furniture including Ames chairs—I thought, "Oh, boy, if the old gang could see me now!"

I quickly got ready and hurried down to begin my speech. When I was finished speaking and returned to my room, I put the mystery together. Prime Minister Begin was entering the suite down the hall from mine. Apparently Mr. Scott had enough credibility that he had cleared me with security.

The next day I stopped to thank him for his effort and kindness and tell him how much I enjoyed the suite. He then told me that his son, unfortunately, died and was never able to finish medical school.

Everybody has a story, so be nice to them all.

Caesar Salad Adventure

In the mid-nineties, we knew that Fred was in need of a kidney transplant. So I took him to a "promise all" medical clinic in Tijuana, Mexico. By promise all I mean that they promise you everything and whether they deliver it or not is a matter of speculation. We were that desperate. Many movie stars had gone there and it had received a lot of publicity. So we went.

We soon realized that this was not going to be the solution to Fred's problem. So to divert ourselves, one afternoon we stopped by Caesar's Hotel and Restaurant, where Caesar Cardini, an

Italian restaurateur and owner of the downtown establishment, had invented and perfected the Caesar Salad.

His salad dressing had become a favorite of his customers around 1932. His brother, Alex, was a World War I ace pilot in the Italian Air Force, and in a tribute to the pilots at nearby San Diego airbase, Alex took Caesar's salad dressing, modified it with other ingredients and called it Aviator's Salad. But that name never took and for all time it became known as Caesar Salad.

Here is that secret recipe with some of my own modifications:

CAESAR SALAD

Secrets:

Place cloves of garlic in your bottle of olive oil as soon as you get it from the store. Keep for a month to add flavor.

Make your own croutons.

Spin dry romaine lettuce and place in refrigerator. Lettuce must be dry and cold. Break into bite size pieces. A knife should never be necessary to eat a salad.

Croutons

Preheat oven to 400 degrees F. Put six half-inch thick slices of French bread onto an ungreased baking sheet and bake until crisp. (I use San Francisco sourdough if I have it.) Brush with 1-1/2 tablespoons of olive oil and return to oven to brown, about 15 minutes. Crush three cloves of garlic and six anchovy filets and gradually add one tablespoon oil. Spread this mixture onto the bread slices, cut into small cubes and set aside.

2 or 3 garlic cloves

2 Tablespoons Dijon mustard

Anchovies

¼ cup olive oil

6 Tablespoons salad oil

3-1/2 teaspoons lemon or lime juice

Pepper, freshly ground

1 teaspoon Tabasco

1 Tablespoon Worcestershire sauce

1 or 2 coddled eggs (Boil water and remove from heat. Add eggs for two minutes. Can be done ahead.)

2 cups croutons

2/3 cups Parmesan cheese, grated

1 head Romaine lettuce

½ cup bacon, cooked and chopped (optional)

1 Tablespoon Balsamic vinegar

In large bowl crush garlic cloves, Dijon mustard and several anchovies and make a paste. Add oils, lemon or lime juice, Worcestershire sauce, pepper and eggs. Add lettuce and start tossing. Continue tossing and add Parmesan cheese and croutons. Toss thoroughly. Serve on a flat plate. Add freshly ground pepper on top of each.

I place several orange and yellow nasturtium flowers on top of the salad. The flowers are edible and have a slight peppery taste.

Serve with a roll, cookie and coffee and have a great meal.

One for Fred
and
One for Me

Picture this. It's 1966 and I'm a novice skier, pushing forty, staring down a 10,822 foot peak at Purgatory Village ski slopes near Durango, Colorado. I'm alone and terrified that I'll never make it down the mountain in one piece. As I linger, my knees quaking as I struggle to breathe calmly, a cute young coed in her early twenties, looking fit and confident, slides off the chair lift. Side by side we survey the magnificent view.

"There's only one way to get off this mountain and that's down," I moan nervously.

"Unfortunately, you're right." I detect an accent in her chipper reply.

Waiting for my heart rate to drop below heart attack level, I stall for time. "Do you ski where you grew up?"

"No, in Belgium it's flat."

"What are you doing in Colorado?" I asked. Anything to keep the conversation going.

"I've just spent a year as a nanny in Philadelphia and now I guess I'll return home to pursue my career. But I'd really like to stay in the U. S. and study English."

She starts down the hill and I follow. I needed a witness to my demise. But she's flying down the slope.

"Hey, don't go so fast," I pleaded. "Come home to Oklahoma with me. I'll send you to our University to study English if you'll help me with my three kids while I finish the research grant I'm writing. The person who was helping me just quit."

"OK," she yelled, looking straight ahead.

"Young lady, I'm not kidding,"

"Neither am I."

"Great. I'll meet you at the restaurant counter if I make it down alive."

At lunch, Alicia met my husband and my three teenagers. I met her older brother, and her New Mexico host, a state senator. We looked each other over and my kids whispered, "Mom, we need her in the family." A week later Alicia arrived in Oklahoma City by bus, enrolled in college, settled into our guest house and learned the children's routine. Every night the four of them did homework and I helped Alicia with her papers.

Alicia stayed with us for a semester, moved to New York for a short time and then returned for another stay. I helped her set up a fashion design business and she moved across town. Life went on as it does for us all, with the usual twists and turns on the trail. Alicia married an American, moved to Texas, then to Colorado and New Mexico. We passed in and out of each other's lives. At times we would lose track of each other for several years; then one of us would make the effort to find the other. Along the way, we both divorced. Alicia returned to Texas and I settled in California. When Alicia tracked me down twelve years ago, I had remarried. During her phone call, she said she was thinking about forming a new business and wanted some advice. When she visited during a business trip some months later, she and my new husband Fred got along famously. My life was settled now, but Alicia was still out on the trails. She would visit us in our California and Pennsylvania homes and stay in our Pennsylvania home when we were away.

About five years ago, when Fred was experiencing renal failure and facing a lifetime of dialysis, I began an all-out campaign to find him a new kidney. A professional speaker, I'm never hesitant to speak up. So everyone who crossed my path heard all about the living donor plan. The next time Alicia and I talked, I told her about our predicament. Once again Alicia responded to my distress as I stood atop another scary mountain, "I'll give him my kidney. No, I'm not kidding. One kidney for Fred and one for me."

I had such mixed feelings the day Alicia was tested to see if she was a match for Fred. Part of me was thrilled that my husband might get a kidney, while another part of me didn't want my dear friend to take a risk, especially at such an unsettled point in her life. But of course Alicia was a match. After lengthy interviews, and much discussion and soul-searching, the day arrived for the transplant. My two patients sat quietly during the long pre-dawn drive to the University of California Hospital. "You can still back out, gang," I chattered nervously. "If it were later in the day, I'd just drive us to a movie and skip this destination."

I shuttled back and forth between their rooms as they prepped the patients for surgery. Alicia called her eighty-eight year old mother in Belgium. Suddenly her mother interrupted their amiable chat. "Alicia, I have been talking about myself this whole time. What are you going to do today?" Not wanting to worry her widowed mother, Alicia has never told her about her amazing gift.

"Oh, I have an important meeting soon, so I have to say goodbye now. I love you." Waiting outside the side-by-side operating rooms, we laughed and joked as Fred and Alicia held hands between their gurneys. It turned out that the nurse on duty had just returned from a

vacation to her homeland in Belgium, so she and Alicia chatted away in Flemish as she was wheeled into the operating room. I walked to the lobby to wait, my knees quaking as much as they had when I stood on Purgatory Mountain so many years before.

For the next five days, I traveled back and forth between the rooms. When I finally drove home at 10:00 p.m. each night, I'd bake brownies for the hospital staff so that the next day they would stop in the rooms often for a treat. We became the party rooms where laughter helped the recovery.

Because of the gift of life given to him by the cute blonde I talked to on the Colorado ski slopes, Fred was given ten more years of a good productive life. A few years after the surgery, before a small gathering in a quaint chapel on Fox Island, Washington, Alicia married a delightful man from Seattle whom she met shortly after the operation. Fred, putting his minister's license to good use, performed the simple, spiritual service that she and her prince charming had written. It's the first time I have seen the minister cry at a wedding. Looking at the three of them at the altar, I felt that finally we had all made it safely down the mountain.

The National Kidney Foundation is the leading organization in the U.S. dedicated to the awareness, prevention and treatment of kidney disease for hundreds of thousands of healthcare professionals, millions of patients and their families, and tens of millions of Americans at risk.

Mindanao

In 2007 I was invited by Dr. Peter Bretan, Jr. to participate in a medical mission on the southern Philippine island of Mindanao. There were about ten of us who had been having weekly meetings in preparation for the trip. Fred had recently received his kidney, so the entire journey was emotional, a true sentimental journey for me.

In Duval City we met with luncheon groups, as well as professional organizations to educate them about how to help their citizens obtain kidney transplants, including how to consider looking for a living donor. We even were fortunate enough to have interviews on several radio shows.

Then in small groups we had the privilege of observing a transplant operation. I had never been in an operating room before. It wasn't modern, but it was clean and adequate for the medical team's needs.

When I went with the doctor the next morning to make rounds, the mother who had given her kidney to help her son was standing by his side and stroking his head. I told her I had witnessed the operation and she hugged me and broke down. We all were shedding tears together.

We were part of a Rotary Club group called Rotaplant. Now it is operating as Life Plant International. It was founded by Dr. Bretan who is a practicing urologist and renal transplant surgeon.

The organization promotes disaster preparedness organ donation and early disease screening worldwide. Life Plant is a continuing project with a strong commitment from communities from Northern California and the Philippines. They provide kidney transplants to needy patients. Dr. Bretan has been donating at least two transplant operations every year. All the medical and non-medical support personnel are also volunteers. Medical doctors in developing countries are provided first hand education in laparoscopic surgery and in kidney transportation. In addition, humanitarian aid in the form of clothing and book donations are transported and distributed at the time of the specific Life Plant missions for the orphans and poor children of Mindanao.

If you want to get involved in helping friends who are having kidney issues, go to: lifeplant. com.

There is also good information on kidney transplants from the National Kidney Foundation at http://www.kidney.org. The Northern California chapter is very active and their main social event is in October each year in San Francisco. Inquire about the Authors Luncheon. You would enjoy it, especially if you can learn how to help someone obtain a living donor kidney. http://www.kidneyca.org.

Look how this helped Fred and our family. He lived an extra productive 10 years because of his transplant. You only need one kidney, so consider sharing. I have helped people obtain the gift of

Life and it is the most rewarding thing I have ever done.

Happy Toes, Bella Luna, and Brownie clubs

Have you ever noticed that people who are sad look downwards? When things are not going right in my life, a trick I use is to paint a "happy face" on my two big toes.

When I was a caregiver for my late husband, and things were not going well, one day I impetuously painted happy faces on my two big toes. When I took off my shoes and socks I said "Hello" to my two Happy Faces, which always lightened my cares. When I showed my preschool grandchildren my Happy Toes, they were quite unsure about it. Was it outside their comfort zone? Or did they think grandma was losing it.

As they have grown older, their sense of humor has also grown, and they have joined me in the Happy Toes Club. I do suggest that if they are in public, they should wiggle their big toe, and it will encourage positive thoughts and might even make them giggle. I like to imagine them giggling in public for no apparent reason.

When I go for medical tests myself, the technicians usually have a comment about my Happy Toes, and it brings a smile to their faces. If you join the Happy Toes Club, it can even be your secret since very few people will ask you to take your shoes off.

Or would you like to join the Bella Luna (beautiful moon) club? I'm the president! Once a month, when the moon is full, several of us call each other on the telephone and whisper, "Bella Luna!" then hang up. That person looks out the window to see the moon in his or her city. That's a signal for my Chicago friend to open her drapes and look out at the moon over Lake Michigan. Or if she calls me first, I look for the moon on San

Francisco Bay. Where do you like to look at the full moon?

Or, you could join the brownie club. Call a friend and share the story of the reaction you got when you gave someone a homemade brownie.

Which of these clubs will you join, or would you rather be an honorary member of all three?

Crumb of Wisdom

"To be seventy years young is sometimes far more cheerful than to be forty years old."

—Oliver Wendell Holmes

Bridgewater, Please Come Back

Crumb of Wisdom

Give more than you take.

—Number Three of Joyce's Lessons

Some years ago, my television personality friend from Hong Kong was visiting. Since I had to be out of town, Aileen and her husband Ken stayed in our home. When I returned, she told me about the hummingbird whom she befriended; every day he drank nectar from the feeder at the kitchen window. Aileen watched him while she washed dishes and cleaned the kitchen.

When I returned, and heard her story about how she loved the hummingbird, I named him "Bridgewater" in honor of Aileen and Ken's last name. For the past eight years, with little variation, Bridgewater leaves my window around December first and returns for my birthday, June 12.

While "in residence" at my kitchen window, Bridgewater has watched me bake brownies for the world. I imagine he has a winter home somewhere in Southern California or Mexico.

As my birthday approaches each year, I keep looking for his return. Perhaps with a hummingbird's longevity, it might even be his heirs who reappear. I get a little nervous waiting for him starting in early June, but he always shows up to help me bake my brownies.

Although he has never enjoyed my brownies, he evidently has an interest in my cause. It is a happy reunion when he appears. I am sure he has never had a brownie crumb, but he does watch me and drink the nectar that I provide.

Bridgewater, hurry home; sometimes I worry that you won't reappear. He does, though, and becomes my seasonal friend. I know that things change, but I still wait for his seasonal return. It is I who wait for him. As I sit here on June 1, I am patiently waiting.

Crumb of Wisdom

"Legends say that hummingbirds float free of time, carrying our hopes for love, joy and celebration. They open our eyes to the wonder of the world and inspire us to open our hearts to loved ones and friends."

—Dominique Schurman

Bon Voyage

Crumb of Wisdom

Not all those who wander are lost.

—J.R.R. Tolkein, *The Lord of the Rings*

I was at the point in my business where I was lecturing in many states in the US, but thought, "I really want to see the rest of the world. How can I do this?"

One day when I had an extra hour on my hands, I was standing in the lobby of the Americana Hotel in New York City. I went to the front desk and got about 30 dimes (this is before cell phones) since it costs 10 cents per call to use the pay phone.

I started calling every cruise ship line in the yellow pages (this is before the internet too!) Finally a gentleman answered and I said, "Sir, I would love to lecture on cruise ships. The title of my workshop would be: 'In an hour, double your reading for life.' It would give your business travelers an extra tool in their arsenal.

He replied, "Honey, that sounds like fun, and normally I'd be interested, but we're going out of business tomorrow. However, there's a man in Tenafly, New Jersey, who books speakers for cruise ships. Why don't you call him."

I used my 18th dime to call Leonard Karp in Tenafly.

"Oh, speed reading," he said, "that sounds like a

subject I could use. Could you sail on the QE2 in two weeks?"

I said, "Of course Mr. Karp. Is the QE2 a nice ship?"

He replied, "My dear, it's only the best ship on the high seas."

He went on: "Now here are your instructions. In exchange for doing three lectures each way between New York City and Southampton, England, you and an associate will get all your first class passage paid, as long as you share the same cabin."

I couldn't believe my luck.

He went on, "Meet me at the dock, on September 14th at 2pm. I will be carrying a briefcase with a yellow ribbon tied to the handle. I will have tickets for you and your partner."

In that two-week period I found other speed reading teachers to handle all my domestic lecture obligations. I invited my fairly new husband to accompany me on the trip and told him that a nice man would meet us at the cruise ship terminal, carrying a briefcase with a yellow ribbon and he would have our tickets.

Fred said, "Sounds good. But just in case, I'm going to bring my checkbook and if he doesn't show up, we'll buy a ticket and take that cruise."

On the designated day we arrived at the dock. We were in the midst of so many people it was difficult to find one stranger with a yellow ribbon. Gradually everyone was called to go on board with just a few people remaining in the large terminal. There was no man with a briefcase.

To be honest, we were beginning to worry and Fred was starting to fumble for his checkbook. All at once I saw a man striding to the middle of the room. In his hand he held a briefcase with a yellow ribbon tied around the handle.

We approached the man and I said, "Mr. Karp. I am Joyce Turley and this is my husband, Fred."

He handed Fred a tan envelope with two tickets sticking out of the top and said, "Have a good time."

Before he could walk away, I handed him one of my cookbooks and said, "Here's a small gift for your wife. Tell her the brownie recipe is my favorite."

When we got to our cabin, Fred and I hugged each other and sighed as if we'd just won the lottery.

We had a marvelous time going to Southampton, staying overnight at Mrs. McKetchum's boarding house. This was called a turnaround trip and all passengers had to vacate the ship for 24 hours after arrival.

On the return trip, we were invited to a special party with Lady Bird Johnson and other special guests. We really were treated like celebrities. And we loved it. I couldn't wait to do it again.

However a month went by and I'd had no word from Mr. Karp. I finally got my nerve up and called him.

"Mr. Karp. I'm used to getting evaluations when I give seminars. Did you get any feedback from my lectures?" I held my breath.

"Yes, Mrs. Turley…and it was all positive. Could you or one of your staff go to the Caribbean next week?"

And just like that we started a long-term relationship. Eventually I ended up placing 105 teachers on cruises around the world during a 14-year period. Their families also benefitted since they could take one person with them each time.

When the SS Norway got out of dry dock in Europe, I was flattered when Mr. Karp asked me to give a lecture on the transcontinental maiden voyage of this beautiful refurbished ship. It was a very big deal. The King of Norway and many Norwegian dignitaries were on this ship for the trip to New York City. A limo picked Fred and me up in Southampton, along with Flip Wilson, the comedian, and Jimmy Kirkwood, who wrote "A Chorus Line". It was almost a fantasy with such star power sitting next to us.

But the dignitaries must have liked my class. After this maiden voyage we were then hired to do speed reading every Saturday afternoon from Miami to the Caribbean. This lasted for about 8 years. So all of my teachers and friends had a wonderful opportunity because of my 18th dime.

Crumb of Wisdom

"Just because you are wandering, doesn't mean you're lost."

—Joyce Turley

Fred the Assistant

Crumb of Wisdom

Things aren't important; experiences and contributions are.

—Number Four of Joyce's Lessons

When I married my second husband, Fred, he was already a very successful entrepreneur and certainly could have paid for his own cruise ship ticket. But it was fun for me to be able to treat him to something exciting where my hard work helped us to go. Ultimately he joined me on three-fourths of the 27 cruises around the world.

The person who accompanied any teacher was called The Assistant and was tasked with making sure the attendees were comfortable.

Fred disliked bartering for anything, but in this case he made an exception and good-naturedly followed my instructions and put up with my star status.

"Fred, will you please give this lady a handout."

"Fred, could you find a chair for Mr. Owens?"

"Fred, we need some pencils up here, please."

Later in the day the passengers would politely nod and say hello to me, not calling me by name, but they would enthusiastically say, "Hi, Fred, how are you?" to him, who they had obviously bonded with during the class. He became the star assistant.

Maybe they remembered his name because I called it out so much during the lecture. Or maybe they just saw in him what had attracted me to him in the first place. His energy, his respect for women in business, his entrepreneurial spirit, and his charm.

He's the one that guided me on all the shore tours at each port of call, since he was a history buff and often knew a lot about each place we visited. Wasn't this an example of giving each other a metaphorical brownie? I gave him a sweet treat of a cruise and he acted as my personal cruise director when we went ashore as well as my highly overqualified assistant during my lectures.

Crumb of Wisdom

Find a spouse who is smart and creative, so you can grow old together.

At the marriage altar, say, "I do!" and not "He'll do" or "She'll do."

—Number Five of Joyce's Lessons

Hong Kong

My dear friend from Hong Kong, the talk show host, loves to receive a box of brownies from me. She never has cooked since they lived in places with maids all of their lives. I do send the Chinese, Thai, Philippine, Japanese and Burmese maids the recipe, so it has become an international message. When I met the maids in Hong Kong, they presented sample foods from their homeland to me. They call me the "brownie lady" from America. I explained to them that brownies are strictly American, having been invented at the turn of the 19th Century. Brownies became extremely popular during the first half of the 20th century.

One of my favorite things to do in Hong Kong is to visit the delightful Foreign Correspondents Club, especially at happy hour. It is here that I meet such charming world writers. One member, Clara, was a very young correspondent in 1939 for the BBC (she is now over 100 years old). She had the distinction of broadcasting late at night: "Hitler has marched into Poland. Ladies and gentlemen, this is the beginning of World War II."

Foreign Correspondents Club in Hong Kong

Here we were, all three of us, on Kennedy Road in Hong Kong seventy-some years later having a brownie together, telling stories about our two countries. Clara and Aileen like to tease me and sent these little jokes about us Yanks:

1. Only in America…can a pizza get to your house faster than an ambulance.

2. Only in America…are there handicap parking places in front of a skating rink.

3. Only in America…do drugstores make the sick walk all the way to the back of the store to get their prescriptions while healthy people can buy cigarettes at the front.

4. Only in America…do people order double cheeseburgers, large fries, and a diet coke.

5. Only in America…do banks leave both doors open and then chain the pens to the counters.

6. Only in America…do we leave cars worth thousands of dollars in the driveway and put our useless junk in

the garage.

7. Only in America...do we use answering machines to screen calls and then have call waiting so we won't miss a call from someone we didn't want to talk to in the first place.

8. Only in America...do we buy hot dogs in packages of ten and buns in packages of eight.

9. Only in America...do we use the word 'politics' to describe the process so well: 'Poli' in Latin meaning 'many' and 'tics' meaning 'bloodsucking creatures.'

10. Only in America...do they have drive-up ATM machines with Braille lettering.

While they are eating their brownies and laughing at us silly Americans, I like to think of them eating this!

Turtle Pie

1 cup evaporated milk

1 cup miniature marshmallows

1 pkg. chocolate or vanilla wafers, crushed

6 oz. chocolate chips

1/4 Teaspoon salt

4 oz. butter

1 qt. vanilla ice cream

Whole pecans or walnut halves as needed

Combine milk, chips, marshmallows and salt in a 2 qt. pan and cook over medium heat until mixture begins to simmer. Stir constantly and simmer slowly for 2 minutes until mixture thickens and coats spoon. Remove and cool. Moisten wafer crumbs with butter and line bottom of a deep 9-inch pie plate with crumbs. Place a layer of vanilla ice cream over crumbs, then a layer of chocolate mixture. Carefully place a second layer of ice cream and then another layer of the chocolate mixture. Top with nuts. Wrap well and freeze until ready to serve. May be topped with whipped cream if desired. In place of wafers, you can use crème filled cookies, but if you do, omit butter as the crème filling will bind the crumbs sufficiently.

Where Does Your Time Go?

Crumb of Wisdom

"Time is too slow for those who wait.
Time is too swift for those who fear.
Too long for those who grieve.
Too short for those who rejoice.
But for those who love—
Time is eternal."

—Van Dyler

A study done by a PR firm in Pittsburgh shows that we spend:

- Seven years in the bathroom

- Six years eating

- Five years waiting in line

- Four years cleaning house

- Two years unsuccessfully trying to call people on the telephone

- One year searching for things

- Eight months opening junk mail

- Six months sitting at red lights

By way of contrast, the average married couple spent only four minutes a day talking to each other.

In the last ten years, have I really spent six months baking brownies? But oh, the nice thoughts I've had, and the happiness it brought me, knowing the love and sweetness I shared with my family, friends, and people all around the world.

Crumb of Wisdom

"This bright new day...complete with 24 hours of opportunities, choices, and attitudes. A perfectly matched set of 1440 minutes. This unique gift, this one day, cannot be exchanged, replaced or refunded. Handle with care. Make the most of it. There is only one to a customer."

—Anonymous

Happy Halloween

There was a knock on the door in my Richmond, Virginia hotel room at 6:00 in the morning.

"Room service," a male voice called out. "I have the breakfast you ordered."

I let him in and he carried the tray to my table. Beside my food there was a little jack-o-lantern. Of course! October 31st.

"Good morning, Madam. And Happy Halloween," he said as he left.

After eating, I scurried down to my rental car and found my way out to an industrial park on the outskirts of town to conduct a speed reading seminar. When I walked into the lobby, the workers were all hurrying towards their offices, fake screaming like they were about to be murdered. There was a huge man in a gorilla suit chasing them around and, arms raised, roaring.

"Look at the monster," one yelled.

"Lady, be careful," another said, looking in my direction.

The gorilla came over to me, but instead of hurting me he put his arm around my shoulder.

I said loudly enough that the crowd could hear, "Big gorilla, do you have a girlfriend?"

He whispered in my ear, "Mrs. Turley, I took your speed reading class last year in D.C. Nice to see you again. Are you still making your brownies?"

I laughed at the impact my brownies had made all the way here in the south.

Everyone went back to their offices pretending

they were scared. And that was the beginning of a happy Halloween. I never found out the identity of that former student in the gorilla suit. If he is reading this and contacts me, I will send him a box of brownies. I hear they are a favorite staple of gorilla cuisine.

Coffee, Tea or Me

Two years after my initial voyage I sailed into Hong Kong harbor on the QE2 coming from India. I called the American Chamber of Commerce and said, "Look out on the harbor. Do you see the QE2?"

The Coordinator said, 'Oh, yes, isn't she beautiful."

I told her that I was lecturing on speed reading aboard that gracious lady, and asked if I could stop in for ten minutes and tell her about the benefits of this program.

I was with my husband and another couple and their response was, "You are always working. Why do you have to make a business call in beautiful Hong Kong?"

I asked them to go to the Mandarin Hotel bar and have a drink and told them I'd be with them in ten minutes. "I only want to make one call while we're here."

Because of my initiative I ended up giving seminars to multinational companies in Hong Kong for two weeks in the fall and two weeks in the Spring. The contract lasted for 12 years.

After the second year, the Chamber representative asked if I could cover another topic since all the top management in Hong Kong

knew how to speed read now. And I answered, "Of course, my training is in speech therapy and I could give courses in presentation skills."

So I did. This extended my adventure as I presented at major corporations and universities.

During the first course that I did for the Chamber, they asked me to go to the local radio station for an interview to promote the public classes. I really didn't think this was going to be much fun, but I appeared and met the talk show hostess, Aileen Bridgewater. We might as well have been raised in the same family. We immediately became world sisters.

Don't tell anyone, but sometimes Aileen was so tired from her grueling radio schedule she would send me as her representative to cocktail parties and galas at the finest clubs in Hong Kong. I loved it because I met people from all over the world...and sold them on my company, of course!

And to this day we stay in touch by phone at least once a week. And I send her brownies monthly.

One funny story about Aileen and me, Aileen started visiting me in San Francisco a year after I began lecturing in Hong Kong. On one visit, I made her a cup of tea and placed it in front of her soon after her arrival. I asked her, "How is your tea?"

In her beautiful British accent she replied, "Not bad for an American."

I took that as a personal challenge. I sent to England for Ashby tea, I bought a beautiful teapot at the Smithsonian, and I practiced pouring boiling water onto tea leaves, throwing it out, and trying again. I studied the procedure for making a wonderful cup of tea until I had it down pat.

The next time she visited, I said, "Sit down! You're going to have the best cup of tea you've ever had in your life. I've been practicing."

The lovely English lady turned to me and without missing a beat answered, "Oh, you introduced me to the delights of coffee last year, so now I drink that instead of tea."

I dragged her out to the car and took her Starbucks.

Crumb of Wisdom

"Just when I was getting used to yesterday...along came today."

—Unknown

Italian Wedding (or Birthday) Cake

Ingredients:

3 cups granulated sugar

1 cup Crisco (or one section of Crisco in foil wrapper)

6 eggs

3 cups cake flour

¼ teaspoon baking soda

¼ teaspoon salt

1 cup sour cream

1 Tablespoon of lemon abstract (or use almond or cherry liqueur) I use one fresh lemon from my garden!

Cream together the sugar and Crisco. Add eggs, then dry ingredients, and last, the sour cream and lemon flavoring—blending after each addition. Bake in a tube cake pan or angel food pan for 90 minutes at 325°.

Ice with a carton of prepared icing or make a glaze of powdered sugar and lemon or orange juice and pour over cake while still warm.

Keep in refrigerator for weeks or freezer for months.

Have a Brownie Together on the Trail

Two years after recovering from cancer, a special journey was necessary. I traveled to Nepal to walk on a good leg—one that could have possibly been amputated as a result of cancer. My daughter and I hired a driver, which is the best way to go when you are not a seasoned hiker. It was a long day...but I was doing quite well on the recovered leg.

Suddenly a little old lady walked out of the forest and in her language asked, "How old is your client?"

My guide, answered, "Sixty-two. Why do you ask?"

"Why doesn't your client have gray hair?"

I answered, "Come sit on this rock with me, and we will have a brownie together." My daughter removed one of the brownies from our pack and I gave my little lecture.

"In America when we don't want gray hair, we use a bottle to cover up the gray."

She nibbled on her brownie. She didn't say anything for awhile, just chewed. I thought she was really enjoying the heavenly taste of the chocolate, but before taking another bite she said, "Next time bring bottle."

Here were two women from opposite ends of the world discussing a concern of older females. Can this be a start of world peace? Perhaps not, but every bit of peace we can put in the world helps.

The little old lady ate her brownie and said, "I will see you down at the end of the trail."

Unfortunately, she didn't show. However, I felt that she experienced the sweetness we had to offer from a part of the world that she will never know but hopefully will feel that we are all together.

Had breakfast here. Look at their marquee! The world loves brownies. But I'm curious about lasagna brownies. What do you think they taste like? (Restaurant in Dali, China)

Crumb of Wisdom

"Life should be a pattern of experience to savor, not endure."

—Unknown

Put a Palm Tree in Your Yard

A couple we knew came by for brownies and coffee. Our two-story Mediterranean house overlooks the San Francisco Bay from Sausalito to the city itself. The view is breathtaking. Bill and Jane were so impressed they wanted to see the views from every part of the house.

After we reconvened on the deck, Bill said, "We are building a house nearby. And we're so interested in inspecting homes that we like." We all smiled. Then he continued, "Would you believe that Jane wants to plant a mature palm tree in our yard? Do you know how much that would cost? It's absolutely ridiculous!" My smile faltered just a tiny bit.

Jane chimed in and said, "Oh, I know. But I always dreamed of having a palm tree that I could light up with a spotlight at night. It would be so nice to watch for it driving up the hill. But I guess it's just too extravagant, as Bill says."

I did not agree and thought Bill was just being cheap. Why not let his wife have her dream fulfilled. Sure mature palms were expensive. But so was building a house in the San Francisco Bay area. Then I got a flash of inspiration.

"You like our palm tree," I said quietly. "Did you know that one palm tree on a property brings good luck? You both should really consider planting one. Look at the luck we've had since we put ours in."

Bill thought about what I'd said for a minute and then replied, "Well, if you put it that way, I guess we'll have to get one."

Jane's smile was worth the lie I'd just told. Even better than giving her a brownie.

Crumb of Wisdom

"People will believe anything if you whisper it."

—Joyce Turley

Paging Doctor Brownie

Some years ago I had an appointment at a major medical center to get a second opinion on a medical problem. I drove from our Pennsylvania home for three hours to a major metropolitan hospital. I was early for my appointment, so I phoned my good friend, a doctor who practiced there, to see if he wanted to have coffee.

"Doctor, I'm in the lobby and early for an appointment. Thanks so much for arranging the exam. Would you like to meet me for coffee?"

He answered, "I'm sorry, Joyce, I can't. I'm on my way into surgery. But call my wife and say hello while you're here."

"Oh, I'm so disappointed I won't see you," I said. "I brought you brownies."

"I'll be right up," he answered.

I met him on the stairs and he was wearing his scrubs. I handed him the brownies and with the container under his arm he made a quick turnaround and hurried down the steps towards the operating room.

It was just what the doctor ordered!

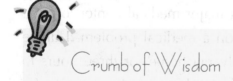

Crumb of Wisdom

VISUALIZE. Then make things happen!

—Number Six of Joyce's Lessons

We Have More Fun

While I was doing my lecture tour in Hong Kong for twelve straight days I worked six hours a day, entertained at night and my schedule was jam packed. There was only one day when I didn't have a class, a Sunday, and my friend Aileen and I decided to go over to Shenzhen, China, so I could see a modern Chinese factory city and get a break from my hectic schedule. Shenzhen was only a one-hour train ride from Hong Kong. The trains were always crowded because people go back and forth often because there are so many factories in Shenzhen.

Even though the trains were crowded to the rafters, they had lace curtains on the windows as testament to the elegance of Chinese tradition.

While we were in Shenzhen, we stayed at the Marco Polo Hotel, one of the leading chains in Asia, and it was amazing. Everyone spoke English. The service was impeccable. The décor in the rooms was very American-like. Everything was top notch, especially the staff.

As the manager was saying goodbye to Aileen and me, four or five of his employees joined us and we all stood around in a circle. At that time, the 1980s, China was experimenting a bit with their communistic views. They had set up 10 southern cities where traditional communist restrictions had been somewhat lightened.

I started the discussion and asked how they felt about this newfound freedom of theirs. One employee said, "I like it. Now I can stroll down the street holding my girlfriend's hand. It's not allowed north of here."

Even though they were being candid, all of them had their hands behind their backs, signifying their reticence to speak poorly of their government. Some traditions die hard. Finally another employee asked, "What is the difference between your American system of government and ours?"

I had to give this some thought because even though this was the 1980s I still had to watch what I said in a communist country. After thinking about it, I slowly answered, "Well, gentlemen, with capitalism we simply have more fun."

They went around the circle, nodding and passing around the phrase, "More fun. More fun. More fun." They didn't pronounce it like a question. It was as if they were tasting the words on their tongues. Seeing how the words felt and sounded. For at least 30 seconds, I was representing my great country. I can't tell you how proud that made me.

I said my goodbyes and we got in line to get on the train for the return trip to Hong Kong. When I went to pay for my ticket, I realized that my wallet was missing. I can't say with certainty whether it was stolen or I dropped it, but in a communist country you can't be without identification. Or money.

Of course I was very upset. Aileen and I went to the police desk. The officer was really nice and approachable, not stern at all. I explained what happened and he was lackadaisical in his response. I guess stolen wallets were a common occurrence. Finally I said to the officer, "I think I'm just going to have to sit down and cry." Aileen rolled her eyes.

But this scared the officer more than anything else I'd said. "No, no cry," he exclaimed. Then he walked us to the front of the train line, which by then was at least a 90-minute wait. Aileen said under her breath, "I can't believe you're pulling this off!"

"See, capitalism IS more fun," I quipped back.

Mr. DeMille, I'm Ready for My Close-up

Since babyhood, I have wanted to become an actress. It's the only thing I've ever really wanted to do. Papa wasn't really a supporter of the idea, but he went along with it somewhat. So I went into Penn State as a freshman majoring in drama. I learned so much and was having the time of my life.

As the cherry on the top of my personal sundae, at the completion of my first year I was offered a summer internship with summer stock in Plymouth, Massachusetts. I was glowing.

Sadly it was not meant to be. Since Papa was a single parent, he simply refused to let his little girl go with those wild actors. So when I returned to Penn State in the fall I gave up my dream and threw in the towel. One day while walking in my building I saw a flyer for a speech and hearing clinic. It looked really interesting. Right then and there I decided, "Why fight City Hall", also known as my Papa, and transferred to a speech therapy major.

I enjoyed speech therapy and my first job was in Cumberland, Maryland, where I was assigned to five one-room schoolhouses. I was known as the "Happy Talk Teacher" and would stand at the classroom door, giving the Happy Talk hand sign from the movie "South Pacific", to indicate it was time for lessons to begin.

Since I only went to each school once or twice a week, during the cold winter months they would offer me the seat of honor around the pot belly stove. When I got married on Memorial Day, they made me little gifts such as pot holders. Some of these children were hungry. But they were that giving. I learned so much from their generosity.

In the spring of that year, I contracted the measles during an outbreak in school and I had to go to the hospital. In the isolation ward there were many children and all night long I heard them sing, "Good Night, Irene." I still find myself automatically humming it once in a while, even to this day.

I had no money with which to check out of the hospital, so Papa had to wire the money from Pennsylvania, paid back the next summer from my salary. In those days there was no such thing as a gift!

After I got married, we traveled with an oil company training program and I taught elementary education in five states because there was such a teacher shortage. I

liked teaching, but I always still dreamed of becoming an actress.

This dream was put on hold over and over again because of little things happening in my life, such as having three children to raise.

Then, at age 80, I became a full-time caretaker for my husband, Fred. Just to get out of the house one night a week, I enrolled in acting school.

After Fred's death I went to my first audition. I didn't get the part, but five days before filming, the producer called me and said the lady who was given the part of 'Grandma' in "Grandma Take Down" couldn't do it. She had a husband who was too nervous about her going to a town for filming that he considered too dangerous.

He asked me if I would be available to take the part. To which I answered, "Of course I'll take it. I've been Second-Hand Rose all my life."

On a very foggy morning at 6:00 I reported for scene one. It was filmed along the beach. I was now an actress!

In compliance with Screen Actors Guild (SAG) rules, they have to provide three hot meals a day for the actors and staff. After breakfast served out of the back of a truck, I headed for the beach to do the scene.

The next day's filming was in Vallejo, California, at a deserted bank. In the movie Grandma robs a bank with a fake Uzi machine gun and gets away with it. I didn't even know what an Uzi was, but no matter.

We filmed 12 hours a day for two days to produce a twenty-minute short that was shown at film festivals around the world. What fun all this was. Finally, I was a movie star, even though I had to carry a gun to do it.

If you want to see me in my glory, go to http://grandmatakedown.com.

My acting career started at the age of 80, with a lead role at the age of 81. Keep watching to see me in a full-length movie. I better hurry!

Crumb of Wisdom

You're never too old to be the person you want to be.

—Mort Broffman

Too Sweet
and
Not Sweet Enough

In 2010 I invited my four grandchildren to spend the summer with me.

With four college-aged kids—two of them were 20 and two were 21—I was very lucky to secure internships (really called volunteer jobs) at the University of California at San Francisco Medical Center. They were all cousins, but had spent very little time together.

The three girls were from Oklahoma City, Seattle, and State College, Pennsylvania. The boy was from Boston.

The bedrooms were rearranged so everybody had a bed, bathroom, and closet space.

As I traveled to the airport for each one, I must admit I had the feeling of "How did I get myself into this!"

They were raised in four different households, with strong likes and dislikes in food. I introduced my brownies for dessert that first night. One said that they were too sweet. Another said that they were not sweet enough. It was downhill from there.

They didn't like anything.

We wrote down a bus schedule and I dropped them off for their 45-minute ride to the medical center. But taking them to the bus every day definitely wore me out. I had an extra car, so finally I assigned them to my brand new red mid-sized Mercedes. I didn't know if that was wise, but it was the best solution I could come up with. They drove the car to the bus stop and parked it there for the day. I told the dealer that I was a little worried about them leaving my car on the highway while they were at work, but he told me not to worry, that red cars were not often stolen since they could be easily spotted on the bridges or highways.

They worked very hard at their assignments so I tried to please them evenings and weekends with special events. We went out to dinner often because they didn't like my cooking. They were very considerate and asked if it was too expensive to go out to dinner every night. I said, with my fingers crossed, "No not at all. Because I have it all worked into the budget." It certainly was easier than hearing complaints. They were always out of money and I know why. They were buying food at the medical center during the day!

We went to a San Francisco Giants baseball game, the movies, concerts, shopping at clothing outlets, and finally to the Gay Pride Parade. My friends really criticized me when I took those "sweet young things" to the parade, but I wanted them to know real San Francisco.

The evenings were quite easy after dinner because they watched my big screen television, cell phones in their hand, computers on their laps. Once in a while they'd even say, "Good night, Grandma."

You can imagine the laundry I did every day, with four young people taking one or two showers daily. They were at the age that when we went to the drug store, we filled up the whole trunk with bottles of toiletries to make them even more appealing to the opposite sex.

Halfway through the summer, we celebrated my 82nd birthday at the local Chinese restaurant.

One weekend we got on a friend's yacht, sailed past the Marin Headlands, and scattered Grandpa Fred's ashes. We decided that it would be a celebration and not a sad event. Fred's favorite song, the one he requested bands play all around the world, was the Beer Barrel Polka. As we spread the ashes, we all urged Fred to roll out the barrel. He would have loved it.

I thought I couldn't wait for the summer to end as I was getting tired. But as I took each one to the airport on their way back to college, I found myself wishing that we had more time together.

Even after a summer of brownies, they still couldn't decide whether they liked them or not.

Since I have eleven grandchildren, to be fair I really should have the other seven out for a summer. But if they call, I think I won't be at home.

PS: After four years I just received an email from grandaughter Allison—"Hi Grandma, Will you send me the brownie recipe again? People keep raving about your brownies so I figured I should try and make them myself again so I can share some of the love!"

Some rewards are slow in coming but always delightful.

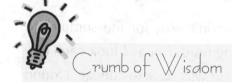

Crumb of Wisdom

If you love somebody enough, you can still hear the laughter after they're gone.

—Anonymous

Easy Souffle

I have served this to as large a group as 75 people and they loved it. If you're not my grandchildren, give it a whirl!

Ingredients:

3 cups French bread, cubed

3 cups ham, cubed

½ pound Old English Cheddar cheese, cubed

3 Tablespoons flour with 1 Tablespoon dry mustard mixed in

3 Tablespoons butter, melted

4 eggs

3 cups milk, mixed with a few drops of Tabasco sauce

Layer in casserole: starting with bread, then ham, cheese, 1/3 of the flour and 1 tablespoon butter. Repeat twice. Slightly beat eggs and milk. Pour over all. Refrigerate overnight.

Bake at 350 degrees the next morning for one hour.

Serves 8

Great for brunch, family, party or after Sunday morning rehearsal.

One Scoop or Fifty?

My friend Christy opened an ice cream shop in Tiburon, California. She had lost her leg as a child when a car jumped the curb and swiped it away while she was walking with her grandma. Now she had a prosthetic leg.

One hot summer day she told me that she needed to be fitted for a new computerized prosthesis, but she didn't know how she could get to the appointment because she had no one to work the store in her place.

"No problem," I said. "I can come in and run the store for you for a couple hours. As a kid I scooped ice cream at my father's store every day."

So off she went and I was in charge. It was quiet and I studied all the toppings and flavors. I felt very organized and in control. I heard a bell ringing in the distance, but I paid it no mind. I should have.

In rushed all the eager school children at once demanding their ice cream treats. Once they filled the shop, the line of kids snaked out the door and wrapped around the block. I simply couldn't scoop fast enough!

Once they gave me their order I further slowed things down by asking a myriad of questions.

"What kind of topping do you want on

your cone?"

"Does Christy charge you extra for two toppings?"

"Would you like your ice cream in a cup instead of a cone?"

"Are you sure you don't want chocolate?"

"Would you add your order up and tell me what you owe me?"

There was a tiny cash register and Christy hadn't left enough change for this fiasco. So I went to my purse and dumped all my change and small bills into the drawer to try to complete each transaction. I was getting comments like, "Could you hurry? Mother is waiting in the car." And, "You're awfully slow. Isn't my ice cream going to melt?"

The only thing I could think of was, Am I in a Lucille Ball comedy sketch...the famous one where she's on the assembly line in the candy factory and things are quickly spiraling out of control. Why do these kids want ice cream anyway? They're going to get fat.

Two hours later when Christy finally returned I heard even more comments like, "Glad to see you, Christy. We missed you!"

After the line finally subsided, Christy said, "Joyce, wouldn't you like to have a nice refreshing ice cream cone after all your hard work?"

"No thank you," I replied. "I think I'll go home and rest."

But I did tell her to tally her money with extra care when the day was over. Between my purse cash and money flying everywhere during the frenzy, I had no idea whether I owed her money or she owed me.

Crumb of Wisdom

"The secret of staying young is to live honestly, eat slowly, and lie about your age."

—Lucille Ball

Wife in Law

Crumb of Wisdom

"The change in perspective astronauts get from looking at the earth from way up high; an even better perspective of life could be gained by exploring inner space."

—Unknown

When I met my first husband in college, he was so smart and charming he seemed like the perfect match for me. Unfortunately that was ultimately not enough and after 21 years and three children, we decided to split up.

Almost immediately he remarried someone more like himself. It must have worked because they were married more than 30 years right up until the day he died.

Even though my first husband and I couldn't continue our union, we respected each other and stayed in touch. Our children tell me today how much they appreciated that we remained friends. And I think our example helped them in their own marriages.

Four months after my second husband, Fred, died, my first husband passed away. When we all went to the funeral in Oklahoma, I looked over at his second wife and thought, "Hey, we loved the same man so we have that in common. I bet we have other things in common too." So I invited her to come out and spend a week in California.

I gave her the royal treatment. I had a limo pick her up at the airport and whisk her away to my home in Tiburon. I introduced her to my friends. We went sight seeing all over San Francisco. We took in shows and ate out often.

We had such a good time, and talked about the nice man that we were both married to.

We started calling each other wife in laws.

As a wife in law we pledged to stay in touch,

visit, talk on the phone and share life lessons, and of course we talk about men and my children, to whom she was very nice.

I feel so lucky that neither of us were angry about the change in our life situation.

At one point in time, we even wanted to start a movement, the Wife in Law Club, so ex-wives and current wives could learn to get along and have a wonderful relationship together. When the opportunity arises, such as when we're with an ex-wife or second wife, we tell them about it and try to soften up some of their pain.

Crumb of Wisdom

Do what you fear and the fear will disappear.

—Number Seven of Joyce's Lessons

Tap Dance Through Life

Crumb of Wisdom

"It's never too late to be what you might have been."

—George Elliot

When I was in first grade my mother signed me up at the YWCA for tap dancing lessons. This was one of the most exciting activities of my life. Since we were so young, it was mainly tap-tap-toe-toe. But finally we did a little dance to the music Tea for Two. I was living in my dream world.

At the end of the eight weeks I brought a bill home saying that to enroll again I needed two dollars.

My mother said, "I'm sorry honey, but we don't have two dollars. You'll just have to quit."

I was completely heartbroken.

Fast forward sixty years later. I met Marilyn Katzman, who gave tours of San Francisco in a fire engine with her husband, Captain Robert. Marilyn had been a child star in Hollywood, and had the distinction of tap dancing on top of the Golden Gate Bridge tower.

After each tour, the Captain would park the fire engine and Marilyn would tap dance for the passengers. I took their tour at least ten times and told the whole world about them. I also gave them and their customers brownies from time to time.

In fact one time I was driving by the fire engine on the streets of San Francisco and Marilyn yelled out, "There goes the brownie lady of San Francisco!"

One day, after seeing Marilyn tap dancing, I mentioned that I had always wanted to tap dance, but that I had to quit my lessons early in life because during the depression we didn't have two dollars for them.

"It's on my bucket list to learn," I told her.

Marilyn was so sad that I had missed out on becoming a real tap dancer because she enjoyed it so much. She reached into the storage area at Fisherman's Wharf where they parked the fire truck and drew out a package. "Here are some red tap shoes," she said. "Why don't you break them in? And then we'll have a lesson. But do hang on to something when you begin."

At first I was speechless. Then I asked, "Marilyn, how much will you charge me for these lessons?"

To which she chuckled and replied, "I'll give you a discount from that old YWCA price of $2. Can you afford that?"

Eventually Marilyn and Robert sold the business and moved to Hawaii. So when I go to visit them there, I'll bring my tap shoes instead of a hula skirt. Maybe I'll even become a famous tap dancer. Why not?

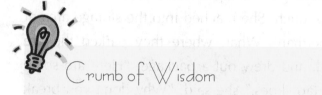

Crumb of Wisdom

"If opportunity doesn't knock, build a door."

—Anonymous

We Speak English

Sailing into Sri Lanka on the QE2 with temperatures hovering around 100 degrees, palm fronds drooping, tropical aromas smoldering in the sun, many drivers were barking "We speak English. We speak English. Go with us."

We had come to Sri Lanka for a very specific purpose. I had studied under the professor who was Maria Montessori's right hand assistant, Lena Wikramaratne. Lena had come to Oklahoma City to teach Montessori methods and, amid fierce competition, I was lucky enough to be selected to be in her class. We were here to see Sri Lanka's Montessori school.

Since we legitimately wanted to do some research, it was essential that we have an English-speaking guide, as the school was not in the tourist district.

So I went up to each driver and said, "Did you enjoy the snow storm this morning?" Most of them would answer, "Yes. Yes. Speak English. Go with us."

Obviously they didn't.

But we finally found one driver who looked confused and asked what I meant about snowstorms at the equator. We went with him.

He took us right to the school. It was an honor to see it, and despite the scorching heat and humidity, it was worth the effort.

We're all asked silly questions at different times in our lives. It's the answers that matter.

Crumb of Wisdom

"When you're curious you find lots of interesting things to do."

—Walt Disney

Sentimental Journey

Several years ago, daughter Kim, granddaughter Allison and I joined the Commonwealth Club's group trip to Cuba. It was not your average family vacation. About 20 of us from the San Francisco Bay area had the privilege of meeting with guest speakers every day to learn about art, dance, medicine, history, education, religion and the economy.

But lest you think this was dullsville, the object was an exchange of ideas and information and we had a blast.

We explored old city Havana in vintage cars, ours was a 1958 Chevy convertible, and saw some amazing architecture. We met with farmers all over Havana and learned about their organic vegetable programs and their dedication to healthy eating. We visited an artist's community project in the Vinales Valley and observed how small private enterprises were growing all throughout the island.

We took a tour of the Fine Arts museum with a historian who explained how Cuba's politics and social concerns are communicated through art. And we even toured a cigar factory and Allison and Kim smoked theirs.

This was all a sentimental journey for me because in 1958, the same year as that Chevy convertible, my first husband and I had vacationed in Havana. What a difference between those two worlds.

I once again sat in the Floridita Bar where Hemmingway spent many a fine hour. The girls asked if I'd seen this or that before and if it was the same. Alas, things had fallen into a sad shabbiness from the magical paradise we'd experienced 55 years previously. It was a shame that this beautiful

city had not been cared for over the years. I'm sure the girls will return one day and I'm hoping they will once again see the shining city I saw back in my youth.

The people were warm, interesting, curious, sharing and gentle. At least that hadn't changed from prior times. And I learned how to make...

The Perfect Daiquiri (Floridita Bar)

1 can frozen lime juice

1 can rum (use empty frozen lime juice can)

Crushed ice

2 tablespoons of powdered sugar

Put all ingredients in blender and blend for a few minutes.

Serve in a cocktail glass.

Great when served with a brownie or two!

Crumb of Wisdom

"There are no foreign lands, it's only the traveler who is foreign."

—Unknown

The Cuddly Curmudgeon

When granddaughter Allison was visiting from Oklahoma City at about age four, Grandpa Fred was being disagreeable about something. My answer to Allison was, "Honey, don't pay attention to grandpa, he's had a funectomy. I now call him a curmudgeon."

Allison went back home and during show and tell at school she said, "I went to California to visit my grandma and grandpa and made brownies with grandma. But my grandpa was a curmudgeon."

I heard about it and it bothered me that I had inadvertently spread this image of Fred to another state. So I called Allison.

"Honey, your grandpa may be a curmudgeon, but he's a cuddly curmudgeon."

She seemed okay with that.

This inspired me to start telling cuddly curmudgeon children's stories. One day I'll write them down. Do you have a cuddly curmudgeon story? Send it to me at spinworld@aol.com.

Double Happiness

My wonderful primary care physician in San Francisco, Mei-Ling Fong, has an identical twin: her sister, Mai-Lai.

Their story started when their mother and father left Hong Kong to go to work in Oklahoma City for Mr. Fong's brother. The couple already had a four-year-old boy and were expecting a baby in three months, which turned out to be identical twin girls.

After a few years, Mr. Fong opened his own Chinese restaurant, the Hong Kong Restaurant, and when the girls were ten years old, they worked there every night after school. They looked so much alike that one would take the order, go through the swinging doors, just as the other sister would come out of the kitchen through the same swinging doors. It fooled many a customer into thinking that one girl was super-efficient and quite the waitress.

They didn't serve brownies in the restaurant at that time, but I'm sure the present owners would consider it.

The girls graduated from Putnam City High School in Oklahoma and then went on to Pepperdine University in Malibu, California, graduate school at Harvard, and finally they both received medical degrees from the University of Oklahoma.

Both completed their residency in internal medicine and now they are in private practice together in San Francisco. Dr. Fong has gone into a concierge practice and Mai-Lai has stayed with her traditional practice. I don't think they have any swinging doors in their office, but I'm sure all their patients are just as amazed at their skills today.

When I first began going to Mei-Ling, I could only tell the doctors apart because she was pregnant.

They both have two children now, American husbands, and see each other daily. And the best part? They're hooked on my brownies. What a ringing endorsement for the healthy quality of brownies.

They visit my home with their families. We of course have the bond of Oklahoma City roots, where their parents still reside. And I always have brownies for their parents.

When I go back to Oklahoma City, I get together with Mr. and Mrs. Fong. And when they're in San Francisco, we connect.

It's such a nice bond and our motto seems to be, "Until further notice…celebrate everything."

In the Chinese culture, the older girl (by three minutes) keeps the family name (Fong). The second girl can take her married name (Lucas). So it's Mei-Ling Fong and Mai-Lai Lucas.

Their older brother, now in his fifties, is severely handicapped and has never talked. However, a few years ago the girls' parents couldn't get out to visit Dennis in his supervised facility because of the inclement weather. They usually visited once or twice a week. After three weeks, when they finally were able to visit their precious son, as soon as he saw them he called out "Papa" in Chinese. It is the only word he has ever spoken. Oh, the power of love.

Crumb of Wisdom

If you like what you're doing,

You'll never work a day in your life.

—Number Eight of Joyce's Lessons

Favorite Day of the Week

I've asked a lot of people to tell me their favorite day of the week and why. Here are some of the answers.

Fred Nicholas liked Monday mornings. It was a new week and he could get a lot done. This is a Type A achiever personality.

Some say they like Wednesdays because they can see how much work they've accomplished and they still have time to do more.

A lot say they like Fridays because the work week is over and they can relax and have fun with friends.

I'm trying to start "Dress Up Friday". Don't you think it would be fun to see what people wear out to enjoy Friday nights during workdays too?

Next I'm going to ask people about their favorite month. What's yours?

Crumb of Wisdom

Honor yourself.

Make the choice to love and value yourself. When you create happiness in your life, you create happy energy that people are drawn to.

Treat yourself like someone special. You are!

—Number Nine of Joyce's Lessons

Saying Hello

At Mount Nittany Medical Center in State College Pennsylvania, once in a while I'm there visiting a patient, delivering brownies, or browsing their gift shop. I find that hospital gift shops are wonderful because the buyer spends so much time looking for unique items.

One of the best things about this hospital is that every time a baby is born, they play six bars of Brahms lullaby over the public address system, and everyone sighs…Ahhh, a new baby.

What a wonderful way for a baby to be introduced to the world. Everybody's on your side. Let's hope the positivity continues.

LULLABY
Johannes Brahms

Crumb of Wisdom

"Babies are such a nice way to start people."

—Don Herold

Saying Goodbye

I've sailed out of many ports while teaching on the QE2, and in Naples I would stand on the deck and wave goodbye to hundreds of Italians who would meet every ship and not know anyone on board. They would wave goodbye with tears in their eyes.

Sometime I want to arrive in Naples and see if the hellos are without tears.

How to Make Your Voice Sound Younger

We do so many things to keep our youth—creams, facelifts, exercise, pills. How about the aging voice? Especially on the phone, it's easy to determine the age of the person calling. Here are some exercises I borrowed from the late actor, Vincent Price. We used them in my early teaching days after earning a degree in speech pathology.

YOUR VOICE CAN BE AN ASSET: Everyone can make his or her voice more appealing. There are five major vocal shortcomings. To check up on them in yourself, ask yourself these questions:

"IS MY SPEECH SLURRED RATHER THAN CLEAR?" Do people frequently misunderstand you or ask you to repeat? Say this sentence aloud several times: *"Leaves, frost crisped, break from the trees and fall."* If it makes you feel a little tongue-tied, you are probably lip lazy. Vowels are easy to say, but we can get power and clarity into our speech with consonants. To pronounce these properly, you must use the tongue, lips and teeth energetically.

A good exercise is to spend a few minutes each day in front of a mirror energetically repeating the alphabet, and five minutes whistling. Whistling is a good corrective for lip laziness. Within two months you will begin noticing a change.

If you need to make your enunciation clearer, practice talking the way Gary Cooper did, through clenched teeth. This makes you work your tongue and lips harder. With teeth closed, read aloud, slowly at first then rapidly. Repeat the sentence: *"He thrust three thousand thistles through the thick of his thumb."* You will find you have to exert more power in your breath, and your speech will be more vigorous.

"IS MY VOICE HARSH RATHER THAN AGREEABLE?" Shrill, grating or brassy voices stem from tension in the throat and jaw. Europeans often comment on the harsh voices of American women. (Tension shows up more in a woman's voice.) To relax your throat muscles, slump forward in your chair. Let your head drop, your jaw sag and your arms flop. Slowly and gently roll your head in a circle. Continue circling three minutes. Yawn a few times, opening your mouth wide, and then say such words as *"clock,"* *"squaw,"* *"going,"* and *"slaw."*

For a few minutes every day, concentrate on talking slowly and gently to people, as if talking to a baby or puppy. Gradually, gentleness will pervade in all your talk.

"IS MY VOICE WEAK?" Your diaphragm, the band of muscle a few inches above your midriff, is the bellows that blows fire into your speech and adds *"oomph"* to your personality. If your diaphragm is weak, you probably have a thin, uncertain, shy voice. Put you hand on your diaphragm and say loudly, *"Boomlay, boomlay,*

boomlay, boom." A well-developed diaphragm will really bounce when you say *"boom."*

To give yourself a vigorous diaphragm, perform daily *"deep breathing walks."* Lie on the floor breathing deeply, with a heavy book on your diaphragm. Then shout several times, *"Hay! He! Ha! Hi! Ho! Hoo!"* Then sit up, inhale and blow out through a tiny hole formed by pursed lips. After these exercises, pick up a newspaper and see how long you can read aloud on one breath. As your diaphragm is strengthened, you will be able to read for 15, and later 20, seconds in one breath (25 seconds is excellent.).

It is breath control, though, not merely lung capacity, that gives you an outstanding voice. To check this, hold a lighted candle four inches from your mouth and say, *"Peter Piper picked a peck of pickled peppers."* If you blow out the flame you have poor breath control.

Whispering is an excellent way to develop breath control and voice power. Have a friend stand across the room, and whisper loudly to him. As soon as he can hear clearly, have him move into another room and gradually go as far away as your whisper can reach him.

"IS MY VOICE FLAT RATHER THAN COLORFUL?" Many persons talk in a droning, boring monotone. Select someone who gets a kick out of life to help bring warmth to your voice. Work with them a few hours each week. Laugh out loud, up and down the musical scale, first slowly and then faster and faster. In two months your voice will take on warmth and feeling.

A widespread cause of flatness is talking through the nose in a twangy manner, a common quality in American speech. To check for this defect, hold your nose and say *"meaning."* Notice how strangely muffled it sounds. Feel the vibration. That is because the sounds *"m," "n,"* and *"ng"* (and only those three basic sounds) are resonated mainly in the nose. Say, *"Father Manning."* You should probably feel vibration in your nose only when you say *"Manning."* If any other letters sound muffled, you are probably nasal in your speech.

To stop talking through your nose and add richness to your voice, use your mouth, throat and chest. The farther you open your mouth, the richer, fuller and lower your tones will be. Try saying *"olive"* by opening your lips only slightly.

Now repeat it while really opening your mouth and see the difference. To add vibrancy to your voice, hum your favorite songs at odd moments.

"IS MY VOICE HIGH-PITCHED?" You cannot actually lower your voice, but you can increase the use of your lower register by practicing sounds that can be resonated in the chest, such as *"Alone, alone all, all alone, alone. Alone, alone on a wide, wide sea."*

Joyce Turley

Say, *"Hello, how are you?"* The first time, put your hand on your forehead and pitch your voice toward your hand. Now put your hand on your chest and low-pitch your words to the chest. Notice the greater depth and richness? You can develop a warm lower tone in your voice by breathing more deeply as you talk and by striving to speak softly even when under stress.

A few general suggestions: Join in with group singing. Read classics aloud, for example, the King James Version of the Bible. These will improve your articulation and rhythm. After a month or so of regular practice, your new way of speaking will begin to be automatic. When you sound better, you can't help feeling better. You will enjoy increased respect not only from yourself but also from others.

YOUR VOICE

Your voice and your face are your "public relations" agents. More than any other factors, they serve to establish an image of you in the minds of others. Your face, body and speech are the interpreters of your mind. They reveal your character, the real you, as nothing else can.

A smile, whether it starts in your face, your disposition or your voice, reacts on the other elements and tends to induce a positive, construction complex that makes your attitude and appearance attractive and pleasing.

Your best voice can help bring out your best self. Nature has given us a priceless gift in your voice. It is the means by which you can communicate with others, the medium of your message. It also makes possible understanding and camaraderie.

The essence of your speaking sound is your voice quality. It expresses emotional color. Your voice coloring is what you use to convey your feelings, and it is important that these feelings be positive when you address an audience. Your thoughts are a form of energy that you transmit to others. Through the quality of your voice you actually establish the tone of your relationships with an audience, or with an individual to whom you're speaking.

The primary cause of negative voice quality is tension, emotional or physical tension or even excessive smoking and drinking. Controlling tension is critical to improving your voice quality.

To improve your voice you must learn to become aware of stress, muscle tension and relaxation. The most important recommendation for developing voice quality is to relax your throat while you speak. Think in terms of friendliness, confidence and a desire to communicate. If you relax the tension from your voice, then it is more likely that a pleasing quality of tone will result. Remember that the emotional and vocal colorings you express with your voice can arouse similar emotions in others.

EXERCISES FOR REDUCING VOCAL CONSTRICTION

As you do these exercises, always be certain your jaw and throat muscles are relaxed. Do them for short periods every day, performing only as many repetitions as you can without tiring your vocal mechanism.

Lying on the floor or on a firm mattress, breathe abdominally and exhale slowly through your mouth. Concentrate on relaxing your lips and jaw by allowing them to hang open. Then try to relax your throat. Each time you exhale, the passage of air through your throat and mouth should feel smooth and unobstructed.

While in a sitting position, repeat the above exercise. Then count to five using your full voice. If you sense constriction in your throat, repeat the exercise while lying on your back.

Do the above exercise in a standing position. Eventually you should be able to produce open phonation while counting to 100 and taking in a new breath after each five numbers.

The rate at which you speak is closely associated with your personality. Consequently, it's a difficult aspect of your voice to change, because it relates to how you think and behave; how you live your life. Yet it's important that you avoid speaking either too slowly or too quickly, because either tendency can distort your articulation, limit changes of pitch and alter your voice quality.

If you're a high-pressured person, you probably won't be able to slow down your rate of speech permanently, but you can learn to vary your rate. People live according to patterns or rhythms, usually structured around a workweek and a weekend. Language is also rhythmic. It contains regular beats and pauses. Your language rhythm is an expression of your life's rhythm. If you're a slow speaker, you can consciously vary your rate to increase speed. Your speaking rate is similar to your rate while reading aloud. A slow speaker reads about 120 words per minute, while a fast speaker reads more than 190 words per minutes.

If you're a fast speaker (over 150 words per minute), take a full two seconds to say each of the following words:

droopy	sputter	fluffy
snowflake	roar	murmur
hush	sluggish	crash
grisly	happy	merry
grumble	rumble	lover
passion	rustle	lonely
delicious	gloomy	luscious
lovely	stretch	moan
stroll	glimmer	

If you're a slow speaker (less than 120 words per minute), say each of the following words rapidly:

flick	nit	blip
clip	pip	glint
snit	dip	snap
flit	click	chip
snip	tip	fib
glib	flip	bit

Indistinctness is an especially annoying speech habit. When you speak, it's vital that you be understood. If you mouth your words, swallow them, suppress them or mumble them, people will soon tire of trying to follow your thoughts. Talking through your teeth or a half-opened mouth give virtually the same effect as speaking with a sheet of cardboard in front of your mouth.

The term "articulation" refers to how distinctly you formulate your words when you speak. It includes both how you pronounce individual words and how clearly you create speech sounds.

"Pronunciation" is the formation and utterance of words. It is the product of correct sounds in the sequence of a word. Mispronunciation, on the other hand, is the failure to produce the correct sounds in their proper order; for example, just/ juts, asked/axed, length/lenth, going to/gonna, etc.

"Enunciation" relates to the fullness and clarity of speech sounds. Pronunciation and enunciation combine to form the basis of articulation or the shaping of sounds by the tongue, teeth, palate, lips and nose. Clear articulation requires three conditions:

A. The sound must be accurately formed.

B. The sound must be sufficiently supported by the breath.

C. The sound must be completely finished.

The following exercises should be practiced once, or if possible, twice a day, for as long as is necessary to establish habits of careful articulation.

Read these tongue-twisters aloud, gradually increasing your speed as your articulation attains sureness and precision:

A. "Willis wouldn't walk willingly within winding windows."

B. "Silly Sally sang and simpered, simpered, and smiled and sang sillily to simple Sue."

C. "Linger longer, Lemuel Lister, lilting limitless lullabies."

D. "She sells sea shells. Shall Sally sell sea shells?"

E. "Many a wit is not a whit wittier than Whittier."

F. "Are our cars here?"

G. "Fuzzy-Wuzzy was a bear; Fuzzy-Wuzzy lost his hair. Fuzzy-Wuzzy wasn't very fuzzy, was he?"

H. "Around and round the rugged rock the ragged rascal ran."

I. "Sam Slick sawed six slippery sticks."

Read the following words to a person standing on the other side of the room and standing with your backs to each other, clearly enough so that he or she will be able to distinguish readily the paired terms:

accepted/excepted

adapt/adopt

affect/effect

amplitude/aptitude

ascent/accent

ate/hate

booths/booze

consolation/consultation

different/diffident

disillusion/dissolution

exalt/exult

foreboding/forbidding

glacier/glazier

immorality/immortality

pictures/pitchers

pleasantly/pleasantry

practical/practicable

precede/proceed

scold/sold

secede/succeed

sects/sex

seminary/cemetery

since/sins

specter/scepter

stirred/third

wandered/wondered

weather/whether

willow/mellow

And: most important of all, get to your optimum pitch by humming, "Um-hmm, um-hmm," as if you are agreeing with a friend. Then say, "How are you?" See how pleasant you sound.

Good Presentation Skills Win Brownie Points

I have been in the speaking business for over 40 years. Do I get nervous? You bet I do. In the Book of Lists, public speaking is the top fear people cite—above heights, insects, and even death!

Perhaps we can't completely eliminate the butterflies you get when speaking, but we can make sure that they all fly in the same direction.

As early as 3,000 BC, the Egyptian hieroglyphics had 20 references on how to speak. Mark Anthony had Cicero put to death in The Forum. His hands and head were placed with a nail through his tongue. Attached inscription: "The Tongue of Cicero is finally stilled."

Do you ever have this in mind when you listen to a boring speaker?

Rapport with an audience depends on:

- content (7%)

- vocal (38%)

- non-vocal/body language (55%)

The experts say that 20% of the audience is paying attention, 20% are drifting, and 60% are having sexual fantasies, or wishing they had one of your brownies.

If you're not getting the response you want, change what you are doing.

Preparation is the best substitution for talent—so PRACTICE!

Make it short. Look at the great works:

- Lord's Prayer—56 words

- 23rd Psalm—118 words

- Gettysburg Address—226 words

- Ten Commandments—297 words

When you go to the podium, be sincere, be brief and then be seated, and you'll win many brownie points with your audience.

Are you happy—then notify your face.
SMILE!

Remember—learners retain 10% of what they read, 20% of what they hear, 30% of what they see, 50% of what they see and hear, 70% of what they say, 90% of what they say and do.

So—treat your audience as if you are having coffee or a brownie with them on a one-to-one meeting.

Smile, practice, have fun sharing your information, and you might even consider becoming a professional speaker.

Crumb of Wisdom

"Smile when you answer the phone; a smile is always heard."

—Unknown

The Wabbit

While attending a conference, I heard my name being called out. A woman I knew said, "Did you hear? My partner and I just adopted a beautiful little boy who is two-and-a-half years old. I know your training was in speech pathology, so can I ask you a question? We think our son's speech development is slow. What do you suggest?"

I thought about my early career, and answered with the usual. "Don't worry. Don't give the signal that you think he isn't up to par. Relax. Boys are sometimes a little slower. Plus he's changed households and he's had to make adjustments. He'll come around. Just talk to him a lot, read, and be totally accepting. He'll make fast progress when he is ready."

This ancient advice seemed to appease her. Then I asked, "I bet he says 'wabbit' rather than rabbit."

She thought and thought and said, "No, he doesn't say 'wabbit', he says 'bunny'."

So much for my college years in the speech clinic.

Crumb of Wisdom

"Everyone's good at something and nobody's good at everything."

—Unknown

Make Everyone Feel Important

For several years we had the pleasure of giving speed reading lessons at summer sports camps in California and Nevada. Johnny Wooden, Rick Barry, and Bill Sharman were the guest teachers at the basketball camps.

Johnny Wooden is perhaps one of the most famous coaches of all times. He was the head coach of the UCLA Bruins for decades. He was so supportive of our speed reading programs for his campers as well as his grandchildren.

His motto was: "You cannot have a perfect day unless you do something for someone who can never repay you."

I think of him every time I have to help someone when, actually, I'd rather have been doing something else.

I'd like to add my saying: "You can have a perfect day if you make just one person feel important."

Notice them and tell them you like something about them—even if it's the color of their shoe strings.

Acknowledge them! They are important. Even a smile to a stranger is saying, "You are important."

Better yet, offer them a brownie with a smile.

As Gene Bluhm says, "A smile costs nothing but creates much. It enriches those who receive without impoverishing those who give. It happens in a flash, and the memory of it sometimes lasts forever.

"None are so rich they can get along without it and none are so poor that they can't be enriched by its benefits. It creates happiness in the home, fosters good will in a business and is the countersign of friends.

It is rest to the weary, daylight to the discouraged, sunshine to the sad and nature's best antidote for trouble.

"Yet it cannot be bought, begged, borrowed or stolen, for it is something that is no earthly good to anybody until it is given away. Nobody needs a smile so much as those who have none left to give."

Crumb of Wisdom

Spin the world—and get on!

Work and learn as if you'll live forever.

Live and play as if you'll die tomorrow.

—Number Ten of Joyce's Lessons

Making the Jester Smile

Robin Williams, the talented comedian, lived in Tiburon just down the street from me. We often saw him walking and shopping around town and he always said, "Hello" with a smile when our paths crossed. He knew that I had been a friend of his late mother, Laurie Williams. She was a delightful, pretty woman who had been a "B" actress in her youth.

Whenever I saw Robin we would reminisce and sing Laurie's praises. He loved to hear stories about her.

The last time I ran into Robin was in the AT&T store. We both needed some help with our new phones. As we sat down, I remembered asking, "Robin, did I tell you about the time I bumped into your mom on Christmas Day as she was leaving the Caprice restaurant on the water in Tiburon?" His eyes lit up.

"We were just entering for dinner and your mom said, 'Joyce, I want to show you something.' She slid her hand underneath the sparkling jewels around her neck. "This is the diamond necklace Robin gave me for Christmas. They're real!"

I laughed at her obvious delight and chimed in with, "Laurie, of course they're real. And simply beautiful."

Laurie beamed and said, "I'm not bragging, Joyce. I just wanted to tell you that I think it's wonderful that a son wants to give his mom diamonds!" That made him grin.

He also gave symbolic diamonds to people he met in the form of a smile, his undivided attention, and his time. It's a special gift if a person can make you feel that you are the only person in the world at that moment. Very few can do this. President Clinton was known for this quality.

One night Laurie and I attended an opening for a collection of a famous designer. We both were wearing hats and a reporter asked if Marin women always dressed up like this. I was lost for an answer but Laurie told him without hesitation, "In Marin we are either in jeans or all decked out...no in-between. When I walk into a room I want to say, 'Of course I took time to get ready and just for you.'"

After relating my Laurie stories I said, "Bye, Robin, I loved talking about your dear mother. You know, she adored you."

He yelled after me with a tear in his eye, "I know. Thanks." Oh, the memories he seemed to have for his mom.

Brownie Points: The Recipe

Crumb of Wisdom

"Life is a privilege to be seized and nurtured until every joyful, exasperating, shocking, fulfilling moment has been savored. Then—you go back for seconds."

—San Francisco Mayor Joseph Alioto

"When you go back, have brownies."

—Joyce Turley

semi sweet chocolate Use good
or squares or blend several brands.
ite chocolate for blondies)

1 ½ sticks butter-European style if possible

3 large or medium eggs in blender;

Add one half-cup fresh coconut and liquefy
in blender. (Coconut in clear bag on baking shelf)

1 ½ cups sugar (Pure cane-fine bakers sugar)

1 ½ teaspoon good vanilla. Try to get 100%
pure Madagascar Bourbon Vanilla.

1 cup flour

1 teaspoon cinnamon-From Saigon if possible

Two cups whole or pieces of walnuts—or less
if desired—toasted

2 ozs chopped black walnuts (optional but
preferred.

Microwave chocolate and butter in large
bowl on high for 4 minutes or until melted. In
blender mix eggs, coconut and vanilla and
liquefy. Add to chocolate mixture. Dump in all
other ingredients except black walnuts. Spread

in greased 7 ½ x7 ½ baking dish. Sprinkle top with chopped black walnuts (I line pan with Parchment paper—(Spray pan as well as top of paper with butter or oil) Bake at 350 degrees for 29 minutes. Turn oven off and remove when cool. Cut into squares when cool or best if cut after sitting over night. If you're having a sugar attack, cool in refrigerator for 20 minutes and cut and lift carefully so they won't crumble.

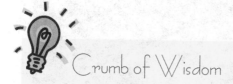

Crumb of Wisdom

The sun has set

The day is done

But, oh, the memories

Joyce's Lessons

(They only took 85 years to learn!)

1. Work where you live, don't live where you work.

2. Never "next-time" anything. There are only so many tomorrows.

3. If you like what you're doing, you'll never work a day in your life.

4. Give more than you take.

5. Things aren't important; experiences and contributions are.

6. Find a spouse who is smart and creative, so you can grow together. At the marriage altar, say, "I do!" and not "He'll do" or "She'll do."

7. Visualize. Then make things happen.

8. Do what you fear and the fear will disappear.

9. Honor yourself. Make the choice to love and value yourself. When you create happiness in your life, you create happy energy that people are drawn to. Treat yourself like someone special. You are!

10. Spin the World...and get on! Work and learn as if you'll live forever. Live and play as if you'll die tomorrow.

"I've had such a good time on earth. I'm going to miss it."

CPSIA information can be obtained
at www.ICGtesting.com
Printed in the USA
FSOW03n0418131215
14171FS